*This guide is dedicated to the amazing CM and VM of Team Adventure. I couldn't be more proud of you both.*

*Always brave. Ever, ever, ever.*

*Forever in my heart - Dad*

## Disclaimer:

The Legend of Zelda: Echoes of Wisdom is a registered trademark of Nintendo. The screenshots and artwork shown in this publication were taken from "The Legend of Zelda: Echoes of Wisdom", a game developed and published by Nintendo.

This educational guide is a 100% independent and unofficial publication which is in no way, licensed, authorized, or endorsed by Nintendo. This guide book is for general information and entertainment purposes only.

Names, brands, and logos mentioned within this publication may be protected by trademark or other intellectual property rights of one or more jurisdictions. It is not implied that there is any commercial, or other relationship, between the publisher and the trademark holder.

This strategy guide's text and layout is Copyright © 2024 by Alpha Strategy Guides.

# TABLE OF CONTENTS

When Nintendo hinted a while ago that maybe it was time to give Zelda a starring role in her own game, they weren't kidding. Based on the same engine used to power the incredible Link's Awakening Remake, Echoes of Wisdom is a beautiful mash-up between the classic-zelda feeling in Link's Awakening, with the crazy, open-ended shenanigans that Breath of the Wild and Tears of the Kingdom are infamous for.

The Echoes you learn can all be be used to bypass the "intended" solution to most (if not nearly all) puzzles in the game. For example, the *Crawtula* spider can be used to skip 90% of a key dungeon, just by climbing certain walls! We cover some of the other amazing things you can do with the 100+ Echoes waiting to be learned in this amazing game.

With our Link's Awakening guide being our best selling (and highest-rated guide to-date), it was only fitting that we took all of the feedback and lessons learned from all of our previous guides, and applied it all to this one - our most comprehensive guide *ever*.

We cover **everything** to get you that coveted 100% completion rate, with tons of maps and tables, our exclusive, tick-able collected boxes for tracking those - hundreds - of collectibles, tricky puzzles made simple, Easter Eggs, and so much more.

We really hope you find our EoW guide helpful (that's its main goal after all). If you do, **please** remember to leave us some feedback where you bought it. We *genuinely* read them all and they truly do make a difference.

Our sincerest gratitude,

The Alpha Strategy Guides team.

# THE TRI ROD

## *There's no Need to Tri-Harder*

Unlike in previous Zelda games (where you played as Link), Zelda doesn't have immediate access to any weapons that allow her to attack enemies directly.

Well, not until she reaches a certain point in the game and, even then, it's all somewhat far more limited than what you're used to (although, it's still a welcome addition it has to be said).

Instead, Zelda has access to a magical stick - The Tri Rod - that allows her to effectively clone specific items and enemies that she encounters on her adventure.

There's a few ways this can be used, somewhat in a similar fashion to Tears of the Kingdom's *Ultrahand* ability.

Let's take a closer look at the key features of this magical staff…

### Clone Me!

Keep an eye out for anything that emits a yellow mist with some triangles around it (especially with items such as pots, beds, etc.).

This indicate that you can learn to clone them (aka: Their "Echo"). Once learned, they cost a set number of stars for you to cast.

For example, let's say that you have a total of four casting triangles available. If you cast three items at one triangle each, you can't then cast another item costing two triangles, as you don't have enough.

Also, trying to cast a fifth item here would de-spawn the first one, potentially putting you in a spot of bother!

If you want to cast more Echoes at once, then you need to level your new friend Tri up! How?

Well, the more Rifts you help save Hyrule from, the more energy your friend Tri will recover, the stronger it becomes, and the more items you can cast once it reaches certain levels (up to a maximum of Level 11, or six triangles).

## Binding

It's also possible to send Tri out to latch (or, "Bind") onto other items that you can lock onto with **ZL**.

Once Tri has Binded onto something then you can often move that item/enemy around with you.

For example, if you see a chest on the other side of a wall, you can often use Bind onto it, and then move it around.

It's worth noting that if you Bind onto something and then go up in elevation, so too does the item (and, in fact, this is **critical** to solving a fair few puzzles in the game)!

You can also use Bind to hold an Echo out in front of you and move it around (somewhat like a shield). Attacking Echoes can be used as longer-range weapons, and you can often pick up an enemy with Bind and drop them into the abyss!

## Reverse Bond

Finally, once you've Binded onto something (like an Echo), pressing **R** will allow Zelda to follow the Binded item's set path.

For example, if the platform moves left-to-right across a large gap, then Binding to it, and then holding **R** to Reverse Bond it, means you'll follow the platform's path!

This is what makes certain Echoes (such as the *Crawtula*) **so** powerful!

You won't use this *quite* as much as Binding to items normally, but it's an awful lot of fun to experiment with different Echoes and enemies to see what Reverse Bond does! Be sure to try it out for yourself!

# OUR TOP TIPS!

## The Benefit of Our Hindsight

Having completed the game 100% a couple of times over now, we thought we'd share some of the coolest tricks we discovered as we messed around trying out all sorts of silly things.

Even *we* were surprised at just how many cool (and hidden) features are in this game. Let's take a look at our favorite ones…

### Power Naps

Did you know that you will carry an Echo that can heal **all** of your health *as often as you want?*

Simply cast an *Old Bed* Echo (it's one of the first Echoes you come across) and simply lay down in it for a couple of seconds. You'll regain half a heart of health.

Laying there *will* recharge all of your health, albeit, more slowly.

You *can* however, get up by pressing **A** the moment your health regenerates, and then **immediately** afterwards, lay down in it again to restart the timer. Repeat this as often as you like for a quicker health top-up!

However, later bed Echoes will regenerate your health *even faster* (and there's also an accessory you can earn in-game that speeds this process up **even more**!).

Combine that accessory with the best bed and you can replenish all of your health in super-fast time!

### Unbreakable Bond

One of the coolest things you can do with the Bind ability is to spawn your strongest attacking Echo, and then hold onto it with Bind.

You can walk around attacking any enemies that dare get close!

## In a Spin

If you want to get around Hyrule much more quickly than just walking everywhere, simply spin with the **R** button.

Not only will Zelda move much more quickly this way, but this spin also works while swimming underwater, it cuts short grass, can deflect some enemy attacks (such as those fired by Octoroks), or even save your health if you catch on fire by putting the flame out!

## Spider-Girl

The *Crawtula* is - probably - the most OP Echo in the game! It may not look like much, but this small spider can climb pretty much **anywhere!**

Want to head to the Northern mountain-ranges at earlier than you're "supposed to"?

Face in the direction you want to travel, make sure there's **no** enemies nearby, and then spawn in a *Crawtula*.

Immediately press **ZL + X** to Bind to the Echo. Now simply hold **R** to watch as the *Crawtula* takes Zelda up the highest cliff-faces without breaking a sweat! Have fun!

## Such a Smoothie

One of the most potent smoothies you can make early-on is the **Sweet Tough Smoothie**, which requires a **Tough Mango and Fresh Milk**.

> **Sweet Tough Smoothie**
> ♥ ♥ ♥ ♥ ♥
> 🛡 Damage Reduction 03:00
> *The texture of the fruit pulp combines with a floral scent in this sweet delight.*

This smoothie not only recovers **10** hearts, but it also provides damage reduction for **3 minutes** on top! Extremely handy to take into any boss battles that you're struggling with.

## Water Way to Go

Believe it or not, but it's possible to pick up an enemy with Bind and then, if there's water nearby and the enemy in question *can't swim*, then they'll simply drown on the spot!

## Crow Kiting

It's possible to use a *Crow* Echo (and a *Meat* Echo) to create a steerable plane of sorts.

If you spawn a *Meat* Echo first, then summon a *Crow* Echo, on the *other side*, Bind to the *Crow* (with **ZL + X**) and then pick up the *Meat* in front of you, and press **R** to **Reverse** Bond.

The *Crow* will start to chase after the Meat, lifting you up in the process (while also carrying you forwards!).

Now, there's a set height limit in this game (as indicated when the screen starts to turn white), but it's a really fun way to travel quickly between areas (especially for those you haven't unlocked a Waypoint for yet).

## Stacked

Echoes are placed on an invisible grid-like system. For example, a *Table* takes up one square. A *Bed*, two, and so on.

So, to create a staircase to reach a higher level early on, you'd normally need more one empty square available in front of you to cast another item on top of it.

However… cast one item first, then push it once, then immediately cast again on the same spot.

Now the items will automatically be stacked for you, saving you time and space (super useful in the very early game!)

## An Eggcellent Deal

While Golden Eggs can be used to make the ultimate Smoothies (usually maxing out the perk of whatever other ingredient you mix with one), they can also be sold for **150 Rupees each**.

If you find 12 of them (*very* easy to do - especially with our guide), then selling all 12 will net you enough Rupees to buy every Accessory Slot from the *Great Fairy* (after paying 100 Rupees to unlock the first slot).

Speaking of the *Great Fairy* and those Accessory Slots…

# THE GREAT FAIRY

One of the great staples of the Zelda series are the legendary Fairies, especially the *Great Fairy*.

She's located in the center of *Lake Hylia* and she can be accessed as soon as you enter the overworld map for the first time.

## Fairly Useful Upgrades

One of the key benefits of speaking with the *Great Fairy* is that, for a price, she'll grant you **one extra accessory slot**.

However, each new accessory slot will cost you *more than the last one!*

It's *definitely* worth saving up the **400** Rupees you need to unlock the first two extra slots (100 for the first, and then 500 for the second slot) at the very beginning.

Here's a look at how the Rupee requirement breaks down:

| Price | No of Slots |
|---|---|
| 100 Rupees | 2 |
| 300 Rupees | 3 |
| 500 Rupees | 4 |
| 1000 Rupees | 5 |

Finally, once you've cleared a specific temple later in the game, a special side quest becomes available for you to complete.

Finally, her shrine **always** has Fairies flying around if you have any empty **Fairy Bottles**…

Great Fairy Shrine

In fact, you'll need a whopping **1900** Rupees to unlock all of the accessory slots!

Jump Height Up

Energy Consumption Reduced Lv. 3

Heart Appearance Up

Extra Energy Appearance Up

**Energy Glove**

Extra Energy Appearance Up

A glove of unknown material. It the likelihood that more energy after defeating dark monsters.

# THE OP ECHO

Did you know that there's a *super secret*, super powerful Echo hidden in the game? In fact, there's only *one* place in the game that gives you a hint that this special Echo even exists!

Not only that, it's actually possible (and potentially worthwhile), grabbing it right at the start of the game (with a bit of cheesing)!

## Before you Start

It's critical to know that this Echo will take a little while to take down (it's tough) and it also costs **seven** triangles to cast. Which means, even if/when you do get early, you'll have to wait until around three quarters of the way through the game to use it.

However, it **kicks ass** and we made sure to use it in the final few battles.

Finally, you can even cheese a *Sword Moblin Lv. 2* AND *Lv. 3* while you're at here (which you can use a *lot* sooner). Ready? Let's go!

## Go to the Eternal Forest

Carefully make your way towards the Northern part of the map and then find the central Warp Point in the forest. Now look South for some **hoove-prints**.

Just like the "follow the sign" puzzle from Link's Awakening, you must **follow these hoove-prints in the direction they're facing**, which will lead you anti-clockwise towards a clearing in the North-east corner.

You'll soon come across an opening and, if you carefully pan your camera up and to the right, you'll see the menacing *Lynel* strutting around the place like it owns it (which it kind-of does)!

If you're going to take this monster on early then you'll have to be cheeky with how you take it on. We recommend one of the two following methods (both rank pretty highly in the "very, very, cheesy" category).

## 1. Using a Crawtula

These spiders aren't even *remotely* strong. In fact, they die in one hit. *However...* what *does* make them useful is the fact that they'll get in a **guaranteed** attack on the Lynel.

Not only that, as they'll climb up and over **any** obstacle in their path, you can basically use a tree (or five) to keep distance between you and the Lynel as you send your eight-legged friend over to get a hit in before it goes poof!

As long as you keep some distance between you and the Lynel, you'll eventually kill it, nabbing the Echo early! Sweet!

## 2. Drown it

Seems harsh, but the Lynel can't swim if its life depended on it (which, it does). The trick here is to lure it down to the nearest body of deep water, which happens to be the **moat of Hyrule Castle**!

The Lynel has a habit of charging your way if it sees you (killing you on the spot if it's the start of the game).

However, as long as you place objects in front of it (such as those good-for-everything *Old Bed Echoes*), then it'll hop over them.

Simply lay a path of beds/objects in your path, making sure the Lynel keeps you in its sight, and hop into the water at the end. It's too stubborn to see the water, and it'll quickly succumb to it's greatest weakness! Gotcha!

# Smoothie Recipes

Ingredients are used to create Smoothies that provide temporary buffs. Here's a complete list of what ingredients are required to make what smoothie and what buff to expect.

**Caution!** Drinking a second Smoothie (while a buff is currently active) **will** override the current buff, removing it *entirely! Be mindful when drinking them!*

| Name | Icon | Recipe | Benefits |
|------|------|--------|----------|
| Apple Radiant Smoothie | | + | Recover five Hearts Glow 01:00 |
| Apple Smoothie | | + | Recovers two Hearts Lightning-Proof for 01:00 |
| Bubble Smoothie | | + | Recovers two Hearts Dive Time Up 01:00 |
| Cactus Smoothie | | + | Recovers two Hearts Fire-Proof 01:00 |
| Climbing Smoothie | | + | Recover two Hearts Wall-Climb Speed Up 01:00 |
| Golden Bubble Smoothie | | + | Recover 20 Hearts Dive Time Up 05:00 |
| Golden Chilly Smoothie | | + | Recovers 20 Hearts Fire-Proof 05:00 |
| Golden Climbing Smoothie | | + | Recover 20 Hearts Wall-Climb Speed Up 05:00 |

| Name | Icon | Recipe | Benefits |
|------|------|--------|----------|
| Golden Electro Smoothie | | + | Recover 20 Hearts Lightning-Proof 05:00 |
| Golden Piping-Hot Smoothie | | + | Recover 20 Hearts Ice-Proof 05:00 |
| Golden Radiant Smoothie | | + | Recover 20 Hearts Glow 05:00 |
| Golden Rapid Smoothie | | + | Recover 20 Hearts Swim Speed Up 05:00 |
| Golden Smoothie | | + | Recovers 20 Hearts |
| Golden Tough Smoothie | | + | Recover 20 Hearts Damage Reduction 05:00 |
| Golden Twisty Smoothie | | + | Recover 20 Hearts Winding Speed Up 05:00 |
| Mango Climbing Smoothie | | + | Recover 15 Hearts Wall-Climb Speed Up 03:00 |
| Mango Twisty Smoothie | | + | Recover 15 Hearts Winding Speed Up 03:00 |
| Milky Bubble Smoothie | | + | Recovers 10 Hearts Dive Time Up 01:00 |
| Milky Climbing Smoothie | | + | Recover 10 Hearts Wall-Climb Speed Up 01:00 |

| Name | Icon | Recipe | Benefits |
|------|------|--------|----------|
| Milky Radiant Smoothie | | + | Recover 10 Hearts Glow 01:00 |
| Milky Rapid Smoothie | | + | Recovers 10 Hearts Swim Speed Up 01:00 |
| Milky Smoothie | | + | Recovers seven Hearts |
| Milky Sweet Smoothie | | + | Recover 15 Hearts Full Energy Recovery |
| Milky Tough Smoothie | | + | Recover 18 Hearts Damage Reduction 01:00 |
| Milky Twisty Smoothie | | + | Recover 13 Hearts Winding Speed Up 01:00 |
| Mixed Apple Smoothie | | + | Recovers five Hearts Lightning-Proof 03:00 |
| Mixed Bubble Smoothie | | + | Recovers five Hearts Dive Time Up 01:00 |
| Mixed Climbing Smoothie | | + | Recover five Hearts Wall-Climb Speed Up 01:00 |
| Mixed Milky Smoothie | | + | Recovers 13 Hearts |
| Mixed Radiant Smoothie | | + | Recover five Hearts Glow 01:00 |

| Name | Icon | Recipe | Benefits |
|------|------|--------|----------|
| Mixed Tough Smoothie | | + | Recover 18 Hearts Damage Reduction 01:00 |
| Mixed Twisty Smoothie | | + | Recover 13 Hearts Winding Speed Up 01:00 |
| Pumpkin Radiant Smoothie | | + | Recover 10 Hearts Dive Time Up 01:00 |
| Radiant Smoothie | | + | Recovers two Hearts Glow 01:00 |
| Rapid Smoothie | | + | Recovers five Hearts Swim Speed Up 01:00 |
| Refreshing Milky Smoothie | | + | Recovers 13 Hearts |
| Refreshing Mixed Smoothie | | + | Recovers seven Hearts |
| Refreshing Smoothie | | + | Recovers five Hearts |
| Salted Apple Smoothie | | + | Full Energy Recovery Lightning-Proof 01:00 |
| Salted Bubble Smoothie | | + | Full Energy Recovery Dive Time Up 01:00 |
| Salted Cactus Smoothie | | + | Half Energy Recovery Fire-Proof 03:00 |

| Name | Icon | Recipe | Benefits |
|------|------|--------|----------|
| Salted Climbing Smoothie | | + | 1/3 Energy Recovery Wall-Climb Speed Up 01:00 |
| Salted Milky Smoothie | | + | Recover 10 Hearts Full Energy Recovery |
| Salted Radiant Smoothie | | + | 3/4 Energy Recovery Glow 01:00 |
| Salted Tough Smoothie | | + | Full Energy Recovery Damage Reduction 01:00 |
| Salted Twisty Smoothie | | + | Full Energy Recovery Winding Speed Up 01:00 |
| Sweet Climbing Smoothie | | + | Recover five Hearts Wall-Climb Speed Up 03:00 |
| Sweet Radiant Smoothie | | + | Recovers five Hearts Glow 03:00 |
| Sweet Refreshing Smoothie | | + | Recovers 10 Hearts |
| Sweet Smoothie | | + | Recovers two Hearts |
| Sweet Tough Smoothie | | + | Recovers 15 Hearts Damage Reduction 03:00 |
| Sweet Twisty Smoothie | | + | Recover 10 Hearts Winding Speed Up 03:00 |

| Name | Icon | Recipe | Benefits |
|------|------|--------|----------|
| Tough Smoothie | | + | Recover seven Hearts Damage Reduction 01:00 |
| Twisty Smoothie | | + | Recover five Hearts Winding Speed Up 01:00 |
| Unfortunate Smoothie | | Everything that uses Monster parts that **doesn't** create a potion! | Recovers half a Heart 1/3 Energy Recovery |
| Warm Mixed Smoothie | | + | 3/4 Energy Recovery Chill-Proof 01:00 |
| Warm Rocktato Smoothie | | + | 1/3 Energy Recovery Chill-Proof 03:00 |
| Warm Smoothie | | + | Half Energy Recovery Chill-Proof 01:00 |

# Potions

Potions are similar to Smoothies, except they only provide a timed buff to an ability and offer **no** health restoration benefits whatsoever. Again, note that using a potion **overrides** any other active buff!

| Name | Icon | Recipe | Benefits |
|------|------|--------|----------|
| Bubble Potion | | + | Dive Time Up 05:00 |
| Chilly Potion | | + | Fire-Proof 05:00 |

| Name | Icon | Recipe | Benefits |
|------|------|--------|----------|
| *Climbing Potion* | | + | Wall-Climb Speed Up 06:00 |
| Electro Potion | | + | *Lightning-Proof 05:00* |
| *Piping-Hot Potion* | | + | *Ice-Proof 05:00* |
| Radiant Potion | | + | *Glow 05:00* |
| Rapid Potion | | + | Swim Speed Up 05:00 |
| Tough Potion | | + | Damage Reduction 05:00 |
| Twisty Potion | | + | Winding Speed Up 05:00 |
| Warming Potion | | + | Chill-Proof 05:00 |

# AMIIBO!

## Unlocking Those Freebies

If you happen to have an amiibo character from the collection, then you can place it on your Switch to unlock some cool rewards at any point in the game.

It's important to note that you won't get any of the cool costume unlocks until *after* finishing the **fourth dungeon!** However, the main functionality will become available *after* exiting *Beach Cave* near the start of the game.

Using your amiibo allowance of **three uses every 24hrs** will merely result in you earning random smoothie ingredients. However, you *can* still scan for ingredients if you've only scanned the amiibo that give clothes drops.

| Unlock | Amiibos Required |
|---|---|
| Red Tunic | Any of the Link Amiibos |
| Blue Attire | Any of the Zelda and Sheik Amiibos |
| Black Cat Clothes | Ganondorf (TotK, SSB), Revali, Daruk, Mipha, Urbosa, Guardian, Bokoblin (BotW) |

Play Tips

Difficulty                    Move

amiibo

Title Screen

You got black cat clothes!

# MAIN QUESTS

## How to Save Hyrule!

This part of our guide covers each of the main story missions that ultimately lead you to the final battle and the ending.

Now, it's important to note that once you reach Hyrule proper (after escaping the dungeon), the same is somewhat semi open to you to explore. It's not as open-ended as Breath of the Wild for example, but it offers a lot more freedom than Link's Awakening ever did.

Therefore, we've documented our *most efficient* path in our 100% playthrough (used for this guide).

However, if you'd rather do things in your own time, we've separated as much of the guide up as we can (especially with the stand-alone lists and tables at the back of the guide).

Finally, don't forget about the *many* side quests that unlock at different points (each with its own reward).

The complete list of the side quests (which become available as you beat key quests throughout the main story) can be found starting on page 222. Let's go!

- *Prologue (aka: The Tutorial)*
- *Prison Break! (Escaping Jail)*
- *The Mysterious Rifts*
- *A Rift in the Gerudo Desert*
- *The Jabul Waters Rift*
- *Searching for Everyone*
- *Chaos at River Zora Village*
- *Rampage in Zora Cove*
- *Southern Gerudo Desert Rift*
- *Ancestor's Cave of Rest Rift*
- *Southern Oasis Ruins Rift*
- *Still Missing*
- *Hyrule Castle*
- *The Rift on Eldin Volcano*
- *Eldin Temple*
- *A Rift in Faron Wetlands*
- *Faron Temple*
- *Rift on Holy Mount Lanayru*
- *Lanayru Temple*
- *The Prime Energy and [Redacted]*
- *Rescuing the Hero Link*

# THE PROLOGUE

## Aka: The Tutorial Area

Once the cut-scene ends, you'll gain control of Link. If you're completely new to the series (then welcome, you're in for one *amazing* treat), take your time to familiarize yourself with the controls by following the on-screen prompts.

Once you're ready, head straight up and onto the elevator. Jump over the blocks on the ground, go up the steps, then head right. Jump the blocks and then get ready for your first fight!

Use **ZL** to bring up your shield and then use your sword (or bow, or even bombs) to take out the two enemies here.

Continue up the stairs and the game now wants to show you how to use Link's infamous **Spin Attack!**

Hold down **Y** and, whilst moving still, position yourself into the middle of the three guards and let go of **Y** to unleash an attack that not only does *twice the damage*, but it also deals this damage to every enemy within a 360 degree range!

> **Top Tip!** For a quicker spin attack, rotate the left stick a full 360 degrees and then press **Y**. You will still perform the same move, but you won't have to wait for the sword to finish charging up first!

Continue on, and use lock-on with **ZL** and your **Bow** (with **X**) to clear out the flying *Keese*.

Start jumping across the gaps, including the broken debris, head into the next room, clear it, then go up the stairs, it's time for the first boss fight!

## 1st Phase

Ganon will teleport around the room. He has a thrusting spear attack that you need to dodge.

Thankfully, he'll hold his arm back for a second, giving you enough time to move, then go to him when he's finished his move and hit him **four times** with your sword to begin the second phase.

## 3rd Phase

This is effectively a repeat of the previous phase. Hit the energy ball back at Ganon three times and then go up and hit Ganon with your sword **ten times** to finish this fight.

## 2nd Phase

Time for the classic back-and-forth with Ganon. Use your sword to hit his energy ball back at him. After three successful hits, he'll move onto the third phase of the battle.

Once he's on his knees, go up and hit him **seven times** with your sword to trigger the next phase.

## The Great Escape

It's time to break free! Once you see Zelda in the cracked crystal, keeping pressing **Y** to smash the crystal open!

As soon as you gain control of Zelda, walk down to the cloak and pick up the **[Swordsman's Cloak]**!

In a gentle nod to the *Metroid* series, it's now time to escape the area before it collapses!

The purple barrier will begin to chase you. Thankfully, this is a very linear scene, but you need to be paying attention regardless.

Run straight down (no need to move left or right here), until you reach the bottom.

Hang a left, and when you see the falling rocks (which *can't* hit you), just start weaving through them as you keep running left.

**Don't stop moving** (even when the stairs break beneath your feet!), and leave through the door at the very end of the room. Nice!

Time for some cut-scenes.

When you get control of Zelda back, feel free to chat with people in the *Hyrule Town*. However, there's not much else to do here, so go up into the castle and speak with the King...

# PRISON BREAK!

## The Blueprints For Escaping

### Escape from Hyrule Castle

Now imprisoned, Zelda is greeted by a familiar yellow spirit named Tri. After a bit of dialogue, Tri gives Zelda the **[Tri Rod]**, unlocking the key gameplay mechanic in the game.

First task: Use the Tri Rod to capture the *Table Echo* from the four-legged table in your cell.

▼ *001/127 Learned!*

Stack the tables to climb onto the wooden shelf and jump over the broken wall into the neighboring cell. Exit through the unlocked door and head left.

### Sneaky Zelda

In the next room, you'll encounter guards. You'll need to sneak past them.

Use the Table Echo to climb on top of the shelving and get past the first guard.

For the next two guards, drop down and box them in, by learning, and then using, the **Wooden Box Echo** to keep them from spotting you.

▼ *002/127 Learned!*

Walk past the two guards chatting about breaking pots (remember this for later), then climb the ladder and capture the *Hyrule Castle Pot Echo*.

▼ *003/127 Learned!*

You can now throw pots to distract the final guards and sneak by them.

After getting past the guards, you'll meet **Impa**, who believes your side of the story. She returns the hood you picked up earlier, which serves as a disguise. Impa also gives you a **[log]** containing a map and a record of Main and Side Quests.

Head up the stairs for a cutscene, triggering your first Main Quest: The Mysterious Rifts.

## Building a Path Out

In the next room, learn and use the **Decorative Shrub Echo** to create a bridge across the bookshelves.

▼ 004/127 Learned! ☐

On the last shelf, learn the **Old Bed Echo** and use it to build a small staircase, allowing you to reach an open window and escape the castle.

▼ 005/127 Learned! ☐

## Outside the Castle

Now outside, make your way to the nearby well. Jump in and you'll enter a side-scrolling underwater section. Swim down to collect the rupees, then climb out of the water.

Use the Bed Echo to help you up a small ledge, and descend the nearby ladder.

Capture the **Boulder Echo** and push the boulder into the water.

▼ 006/127 Learned! ☐

Use the beds or boxes to create a floating path across the water. Then, drop a boulder onto the next set of floating boxes to weigh them down.

Swim down the other side and climb out of the water.

## The Suthorn Prairie

Approach the door at the top of the stairs and a cutscene will trigger.

The rift will expand again, forcing you to run forwards where you have to jump into the rushing water.

You'll be swept away, eventually arriving at the *Suthorn Prairie*, ready to continue your journey onwards.

**Top Tip!** If you lay down in the Old Bed Echo, then you'll - slowly - regain **ALL** of your health! However, you can speed this up by sitting up and laying back down **immediately** after your energy is topped up. Repeat this as often as you like for effectively infinite energy refills!

# THE MYSTERIOUS RIFTS

 Uncovering the Great Mystery

## Suthorn Prairie

After escaping Hyrule Castle, you'll wake up in a sandy cove. Your first task is to capture the **Rock Echo** and head outside to find yourself on the beach.

▽ 007/127 Learned! ☐

Tri will point out an enemy nearby that you can easily defeat by throwing Rocks — once you do, capture the **Zol Echo**.

▽ 008/127 Learned! ☐

Swim into the water for a **Blue Rupee** worth **five Rupees**. However, we still need to fill Zelda's purse, so let's grab a chest with some more in it.

Look up to see a chest on a ledge. Use your Tables and Shrub echoes (or stack a bunch of old beds) to make a platform up to the chest. Open it to find a **Red Rupee** worth a cool **20 Rupees!**

To get past the Sea Urchin enemies, lock-on and throw a Rock at it, don't forget to capture the **Sea Urchin Echo**.

▽ 009/127 Learned! ☐

Now head South across the sea, picking up the rupees in the water along the way, climb up onto the island and you can snag a [Piece of Heart] along the way by using a series of Old Beds to make a long platform to reach it.

Climb onto the rocks and head north, using more beds to bridge the gap where a ladder is broken.

At the top, you'll enter a cave — defeat the Keese inside for a *Keese Echo*.

▼ 010/127 Learned! ☐

Near the climbing wall, climb up, stand by the edge of the platform, and then keeping dropping a boulder onto all of the wooden boxes to reach a second [Piece of Heart].

Once you're done, exit to the right and you'll emerge in *Suthorn Prairie* proper. Follow the path, and just before reaching *Suthorn Village*, use beds to climb up to a treasure chest containing a **Purple Rupee** that's worth **50 rupees**. Nice!

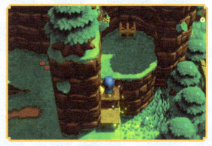

## Suthorn Village

The village is quiet for now, but you can chat with the villagers. They'll mention someone named Link… strange. Check out the houses to find a *Pot Echo* (smash all of the pots and you'll likely find a **Floral Nectar** jar. These are ingredients that are used to make very helpful smoothies later on).

▼ 011/127 Learned! ☐

Next to the *Item Shop,* you can grab the **Trampoline Echo,** which will come in handy later.

▼ *012/127 Learned!*

If you have **80 Rupees** (which you definitely will if you've been following our guide), you can also purchase a [Piece of Heart] from the shop.

♥ *03/40 Collected?*

Before leaving, jump down the well for a chest holding **5 x [floral nectar.]** Sweet! (literally).

Lueberry isn't here at the moment, so when you're done exploring, leave the village from the east. As you exit, capture the **Sign Echo.**

▼ *013/127 Learned!*

## Suthorn Forest

The forest ramps up the difficulty with more enemies lurking about. First things first, unlock your first **Waypoint** for fast travel.

**Top Tip!** You *don't* need to warp from Waypoint to Waypoint. You can, in fact, warp to **any unlocked Waypoint *at any time!*** This will save you *loads* of time getting used to now - trust us on this one!

Keep following the path and you'll come across a chest containing **5 x [Electro Apples]**. If you use Old Beds to climb up the nearby cliff, there's an easy **20 rupees** waiting for you.

Walk further in and enter the cave here. Use a Rock on the new fire-type enemy, an **Ignizol** and capture its Echo.

▼ *014/127 Learned!*

Select this Echo and use it on the Zol and also on the unlit fire to open the door. Inside you'll find a chest, which contains a **[Fairy Bottle]** (the first of four).

Exit the cave and head further into the forest. You'll soon encounter some snakes. Drop a Sea Urchin in front of you for an easy kill. Now go learn the **Rope Echo**.

▼ 015/127 Learned! ☐

Go East a bit towards the row of trees. Use a few Trampolines to get up onto the trees (what used to be a glitch in Link's Awakening, is now an intentional part of the game!). There's a chest nearby with a handy **50 Rupees** in it.

North of the snake area is a cave. Go inside and drop a Sea Urchin on the ground to quickly capture the **Caromadillo Echo** and use it

to clear the boxes on your way around to pick up another **[Piece of Heart]** (this should be your fourth, giving you an extra heart! Nice one!).

▼ 016/127 Learned! ☐

♥ 04/40 Collected? ☐

When you leave the cave, head west for a Spear Moblin. Lock onto it and keep spamming it with *Caromadillos* to earn the **Spear Moblin Echo**.

▼ 017/127 Learned! ☐

Just up ahead there's a pool of water with a *Fairy* in it. Jump into the water and the *Fairy* will **jump into your empty Fairy Bottle!**

What this means is that, should you lose all your hearts, the *Fairy* will automatically restore some of your health, preventing a Game Over.

Keep going until you spot a large mass of purple energy blocking your path.

Go up the pathway and you'll stumble upon a Moblin camp — clear them out with your Caromadillos to claim a chest with **10 x [Refreshing Grapes]** inside. You can also clone the Meat for the *Meat Echo*.

▼ 018/127 Learned! ☐

Past the Moblin camp, walk past the wooden posts and look down, there's a hidden cave covered by two fire Braziers.

▼ 019/127 Learned! ☐

Jump across to them, learn the *Brazier Echo* and then head inside the cave.

Once inside, head up and you'll encounter a new enemy - the *Peahat*.

These are weak to fire, so get its attention, then draw it down to you and once its spinning points go back in, throw an *Ignizol* at it to set it on fire.

Keep this up until it dies and then go learn the - **super helpful** - *Peahat Echo!*

▼ 020/127 Learned! ☐

*Top Tip!* This Echo is really powerful (at least early game). Firstly, if you're locked on to an enemy, it'll match its height and fly over to it and hit it constantly.

Secondly, you can pick it up by a ledge and use it to glide off of cliffs or other similarly high areas down to lower ground! They're awesome!

# STILLED SUTHORN FOREST

## Welcome to the Dark Side...

Welcome to the Still World! You'll be hopping into these rifts throughout Echoes of Wisdom, so it's time to get familiar.

This particular rift is short and straightforward. Just follow the path while listening to Tri's explanations.

There's a cave here with a few enemies if you feel like fighting, but don't forget to break the boxes for some useful items.

A word of caution, the dark flying puddles will make clones of *the last Echoes you used*! So, be **very** careful when approaching them!

Jump across the floating trees and then head into the cave. Jump across the gaps (ignoring the Dark Keese) and stand on the switch to open the door. Jump back across and go through the open door.

In the next room, use your new *Peahat* to make light work of the Dark Zols in the room.

Head out of the cave, go up, then immediately jump right, use the trees sticking out as platforms, collect the **Blue Rupee**, come back down, and proceed left (past the Dark blob).

Keep heading left and you'll soon arrive at the first dungeon in the game - *Suthorn Ruins*. Time to gear up and head inside!

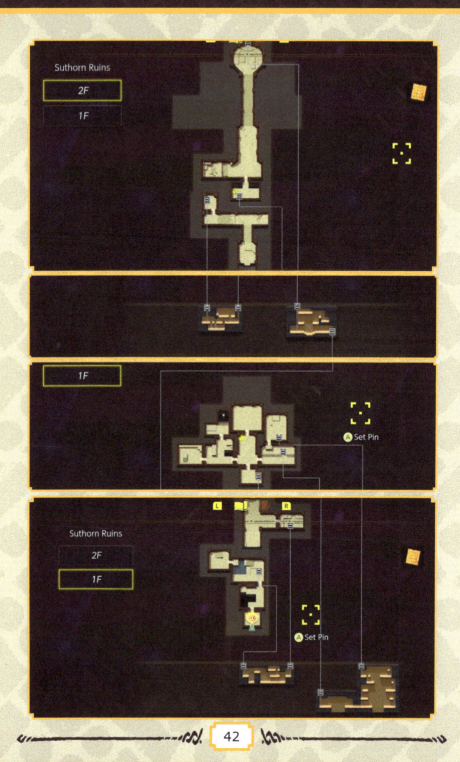

Suthorn Ruins

2F
1F

1F

A Set Pin

Suthorn Ruins

2F
1F

L | R

A Set Pin

When you enter, activate the **Waypoint** and go through the north door. You'll come across a large rock. Tri will explain how to use **Bind** here.

Move the rock forwards with Bind and drop it on top of the switch to unlock the door on the right.

In the next room, Bind the rock again (and then *jump as you move, lifting the rock with you*) to get it up high enough to get to the water to place it in the gap between the platforms.

Climb the slope, cross over the rock, and enter the next room where a chest is buried in the sand.

Use Bind, *and pull back on the control stick* to pull it out and claim **5 x [Radiant Butter]**.

Now, head down the ladder that was hidden by the rock.

Make sure to capture the **Strandtula Echo**. Use this to create spider webs for climbing.

▼ 021/127 Learned! ☐

Climb up and grab the chest at the top of the room for the **[Dungeon Map]**, then exit via the right ladder.

In the next room, use either beds or the Strandtula Echo to get across the gap and continue on.

Go forwards, then right, then up the lift. At the top of the stairs, you'll face a Darknut. Defeat it to obtain the **Darknut Echo**.

▼ 022/127 Learned! ☐

Head left and descend the ladder. Use the Ignizol to light the torches, then Bind the boulder out of the way. Burn down the boxes with the Ignizol to reach the final torch, unlocking the ladder on the right.

You'll emerge in a room with another **Waypoint**. Activate it, then take a look at the four statues on the wall.

The one to the right of the door has a shield. Use **Bind to pull the shield off**, then head through the door. Defeat another Darknut inside and use beds (or your spider) to reach a chest with **50 rupees** on the left side of the room.

Now, head north to face the, rather familiar-looking, mini-boss.

 **BOSS FIGHT: DARK LINK**

### 1st Phase

Immediately upon starting the battle, use **Bind** on Link's shield and pull it away from him, making him *much* easier to hit!

Now switch to your *Caromadillo* Echo, lock onto Link and use it **six times** to send this battle onto phase two.

### 2nd Phase

Run around the large block and then grab Link with **Bind**. Pull him out, pull his shield off of him once again, and further **six hits** with your trusty *Caromadillo* will finish this fight off very quickly.

## You Have the Power!

After the fight, you'll receive the Sword, granting you access to **Swordfighter Form!**

After the cutscene, immediately transform into Swordfighter Form (by pressing UP on the d-pad) and use your sword to destroy the black goo blocking your path. Climb down the ladder to the next section.

At the bottom, use Bind and drag the rock into the dip on the floor.

Climb back up the ladder on the left, cross the gap, and use the Strandtula Echo to climb up to a treasure chest containing the **[Heart Pin]** accessory! Make sure to equip it in the main menu.

Exit to the bottom-right and head through the next door. Inside, activate the **Waypoint** in front of the large door, then leave through the left door.

## Puzzle Rooms

Catch the *Deku Baba Echo* here (by pulling on its head with Bind), then switch to Swordfighter Form to cut through more goo.

023/127 Learned!

Defeat the Deku Babas, the and in the top right corner, clear one last Baba to unlock the doors to the north and west.

Head through the west door first, grab the statue up close with Bind, then walk backwards to the wall, then use the slope to **lift** the statue up onto the switch to the right (because it matches your height - **remember this**), and you'll get a chest worth **50 rupees.**

Now return to the previous room and head north. Use Bind to grab a Deku Baba through the grate and defeat it. Open the chest here for a **[Silver Key]**.

## Final Puzzle

Go back to the main hall with the Waypoint and use the key to unlock the right door. Bind the statue behind the bars to place it on the switch, then head down the ladder.

Here's where you'll learn about **Reverse Bond**.

> **Top Tip!** *Spend the time now to learn how to do this well. Later on, you can use this mechanic to bust the game wide open and use it in conjunction with other Echoes to do some **really** cool and funky tricks!*

Use it to grapple onto the moving platform above and ride it across the room. Keep grappling and walking until you reach the top. A chest here contains **20 rupees**.

Climb the ladder at the top to find another Bind puzzle. Build a bed in front of the switch, then Bind the statue and carry it up onto the bed and jump up to place it on the switch. This will unlock a chest containing the **[Big Key]**!

Now, warp back to the main hall, save your game, and use the key to unlock the **Boss Door**.

## 1st Phase

Immediately lock onto the **Purple Ball** under the boss, **Bind** to it, then pull the ball out.

Switch to Swordfighter mode and hit the purple ball **seven times**. This kicks off phase two.

*Immediately* switch back to regular Zelda to save precious energy.

## 2nd Phase

Once again look for the purple ball on its **right-hand shoulder**. Lock onto it, **Bind** onto it, and quickly move out of the way to dodge its hand attack as you pull backwards to dislodge the ball.

Same as before, switch to Swordfighter mode and hit the purple ball another **seven times** to trigger the third, and final, phase of this fight.

## 3rd Phase

The boss will turn red and the ball is located at the top of its head.

Wait for it to slam the ground (make sure you're not too close to be hit) and then lock on, **Bind** onto it, and *very* quickly pull it out of its head.

However, you may need to dodge its spinning and/or ground punching attacks first.

It takes **14 hits** with your sword to finish this battle, so don't hang around switching to Swordfighter mode and getting up close!

# SEARCHING FOR EVERYONE

 *The Adventure Begins Now...*

## Might Crystals

Along with the **Heart Container**, you'll also acquire your first **5 x [Might Crystals]**. These effectively replace the Secret Seashells hidden in Link's Awakening and, like the Secret Seashells, will be hidden.

There's a whopping **150** to obtain in the whole game, so we've added a way for you to track your collection of those as well!

**005/150 Collected!**

Once you've warped back to the overworld, follow *Minister Lefte* as they walk you to *Luberry's* house.

Luberry will take your **Might Crystals** from you and use them to power up your Swordfighter form sword (among other items later in the game…).

You've conveniently got enough Might Crystals to upgrade your power bar (aka: your "energy"). This upgrades your Swordfighter energy bar from Lv. 1 to Lv. 2 (meaning it'll last a little longer when you use it in battle).

Once you've got it upgraded, you can go be nosy and go downstairs to read Luberry's diary entries, or you can either:

- Explore the world at your own pace. It's now pretty much completely open for you to explore.
- Head to the *Gerudo Desert* to complete that quest.
- Head to *Zora River* to finish that main quest.

As we mentioned in our introduction, we've provided our 100% playthrough in a linear fashion (should you want a fast and efficient way to achieve 100% as well). However, we appreciate you may want to play it a completely different way (because it's so open), so we've still sign-posted the key quest names and we've also effectively duplicated some key information at the back of our guide.

Side Quests, Accessories, Echoes, Piece of Heart, Might Crystals, and Stamp Stands are all logged and mapped out at the very back, so you can still take a look to see what you've missed if you're playing it your own way. We *hope* this strikes a balance between providing detailed help (where it's needed) and leaving you to play it your own way.

Main Quest | Accessory | Heart Piece

Side Quest | Enemy Echo | Might Crystal

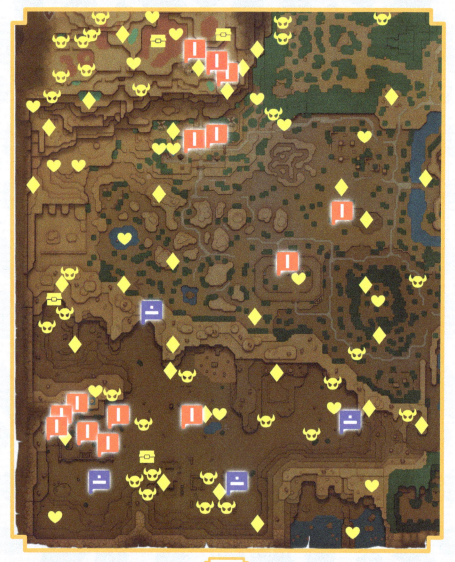

# GERUDO SANCTUM RIFT

 ## Our Just Desserts in the Desert

### En-Route to Gerudo

As soon as you leave Luberry's home, warp to *Waypoint* outside *Suthorn Village* and speak to the old man with the red exclamation mark over his head.

This starts the *Finding the Flying Plant* Side Quest. Because you already have a *Peahat* Echo, make one appear in front of him to immediately finish it, earning you a sweet [Might Crystal] in return!

> **Top Tip!** The Crawtula will climb up pretty much **anything**. Want to reach the mountainous areas now? Well, you can!
>
> Just face the direction you want to travel, press **Y** to spawn one, then **X** to **Bind** to it, and quickly press **R** to initiate a **Reverse Bond**. Zelda will now follow the Crawtula as it keeps climbing until it can't climb no more!
>
> It - very quickly - became one of our most used Echoes in the whole game!

006/150 Collected!

024/127 Learned!

Exit the village via the way you came in, go north at the sign, then travel North-east until you see a new **Waypoint**, activate it.

Continue North into *Suthorn Prairie* and capture what is most one of **the** most overpowered Echoes in the whole game, the *Crawtula Echo*.

It's time to put this Echo to the test. Head up towards the central pillar surrounded by water, and place an Old Bed in the water so it's floating. Now face the pillar head-on and use a *Crawtula* to climb up the pillar to the [Piece of Heart]! Nice!

❤ **05/40 Collected?** ☐

There's a Side Quest nearby - *Up a Wall* - that you can quickly finish. Just kill the two *Moblins* here for a quick win.

Proceed directly West from here and look for a cave by some pillars. Head inside and use the Crawtula's super-powers to climb up the wall to the chest at the top. Open it for a quick **50 Rupees**.

Head South outside the cave and use your *Peahat* to take out the *Octorok* in the water. Jump in and add the **Octorok Echo** to your collection!

▼ **025/127 Learned!** ☐

While you're here, dive down and spin to cut the grass in the middle. There's a *very* sneakily hidden **[Might Crystal]** under one of them!

◆ **007/150 Collected!** ☐

Continue South and there's another pool of water, with a chest on top of a pillar. Clear the *Moblin* here and then climb the pillar however you like, and open the chest for a cool 10 x **[Rock Salt]**.

Drop down, head left, then line yourself up with the lone rock sitting at the top of the rocky wall. Use your *Crawtula* to get up to it easily and lift the rock for the next **[Might Crystal]**!

◆ **008/150 Collected!** ☐

Go up a bit, then lock-on to the *Crow* on the tree stump to your left. Kill it and grab the **Crow Echo** as it drops to the ground.

▼ 026/127 Learned! □

Go South and use Bind on the chest that's sitting up on the tree stump. Lift it off and open it for a cool **50 Rupees**.

Now run North-west and look for a Rock on top of a tree stump. That's a bit odd, isn't it? Clear the area of Crows first, and then use Bind and a Trampoline to grab the [Might Crystal] that appears!

💎 009/150 Collected! □

Drop down, go South, and immediately activate the **Waypoint** at the desert's edge.

## Gerudo Desert

Alright, we've finally made it to the desert itself. As soon as you enter the desert, head north until you hit a wall.

Use a series of beds or a *Crawtula* to climb up the wall towards the cave. Head inside the cave and here you will find a tougher *Caromadillo*.

Use your peahat to attack it from up above. Then go down, And claim your **Caromadillo Lv.2 Echo**.

▼ 027/127 Learned! □

If you want 10 pieces of [Chilly Cactus] (which will help with future Gerudo side quests, head up the nearby ladder and you will find two more Caromadillos in this room.

Use your strongest Echo and once they've both been defeated, open the chest and you will get your Chilly Cactus.

Exit the cave, head west and look out for these new Scorpion enemies. Take them out with your new *Caromadillo* and claim your new Echo. This will be the **Aruroda Echo**.

▼ 028/127 Learned! □

Pull the chest out of the sand and open it up for **20 rupees**. Now use your crotch holder to continue left up the ledges towards the rift.

Now head South-west and then continue towards the West.

You'll see a lone rock. Lift it up and underneath is a [Might Crystal].

🔷 010/150 Collected!

Drop down and you'll be at the *Oasis*. Activate the new **Waypoint** here. Go left and speak with the *Business Scrub* and you now have access to Smoothies!

Mix two Chilly Cactus together for the **Cactus Smoothie**.

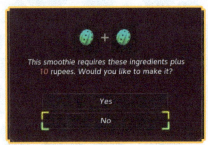

Speak with the nearby Gerudo to start **The Flying Tile** Side Quest. Head inside the tent and capture the **Soft-Bed Echo**. This bed recovers your hearts faster than the Old Bed Echo does!

> **Top Tip!** Remember… get back up **immediately** after your health is topped up and then lay back down again. Keep repeating this (somewhere safe!) until you're OK.

▼ 029/127 Learned! ☐

Speak with the woman here to start the **Mango Rush** mini-game! A full breakdown on how to beat all three difficulty levels can be found on page 242.

The first round is easy if you spin dash around the room cutting the plants down. However, the *Vibrant Seeds* requires more strategy, so head to that page if you want to tackle those two levels now.

If you did the first level, you'll be given some [Tough Mangoes] and if you do the next, harder, challenge, you'll get her [Golden Fan] and 3 x [Might Crystals].

🔷 013/150 Collected! ☐

Head South and get ready to take out an annoying enemy, the ReDead. They shriek and if you're too close, this causes you to freeze on the spot for a while.

▼ *030/127 Learned!* ☐

Lock-on, walk back, and start sending your *Caromadillos* their way! Collect your **ReDead Echo** when it's safe.

Now grab the nearby piranha with **Bind** and hold it in place until your own Echo dispatches it. Learn the *Sand Piranha Echo*.

▼ *031/127 Learned!* ☐

Go North-west and activate the next **Waypoint**. Go right a bit, enter the open doorway and select the **Boulder** Echo. Place these down so they block the air blowing your way.

Once across, go learn the *Gerudo-pot Echo*.

▼ *032/127 Learned!* ☐

Go up the sand ramp, drop a non-moving Echo, and push it up to the Wind-cannon. Learn the *Wind-cannon Echo* as it'll prove very useful later on.

▼ *033/127 Learned!* ☐

Head inside the next room and use the Wind-cannon Echo to blow away the piles of sand. If you pick it up, you can control the direction in which the wind blows (it even pushes back enemies).

Stand on the switch in the left corner, go in the top door and you'll see a new enemy type. Grab one with Bind and use an Echo to take it down. Now go learn the **Tornando Echo**.

▼ 034/127 Learned! □

Clear this room and open the chest for 3 x **[Rocktatoes]**. Now leave the room and head into the right-hand door. Open the chest here for **2 x [Might Crystals!]** Sweet!

◆ 015/150 Collected! □

After leaving the cave, go right and use a *Crawtula* to climb up the wall here to the first of 25 **[Stamp Stands]**!

👤 01/25 Located! □

Note, that for every five Stamp Stands you find, Stamp Guy will give you a reward. A map showing you the location of **every** Stamp Stand can be found on page 280 at the back of our guide.

Head directly South and clear the two piles of sand to reveal a **[Might Crystal]** under one.

◆ 016/150 Collected! □

Head West and pull the chest out of the sand for 10 x **[Chilly Cactus]**. Continue heading West and the chest in the sand here contains **20 Rupees**.

Keep going West until **Tri** talks to you about the Rift. Speak with the Gerudo Guard nearby then get ready to save someone and get rid of some Dark Echoes.

Once she's been saved, speak with **Dohna** and then go to the most South-western corner of the desert. Use the Wind-cannon on the sand in the middle to uncover a **[Piece of Heart]**! Sweet!

❤ 06/40 Collected? □

Go North, drop down and blow away the sand by the cacti to reveal a chest with **50 Rupees** inside.

Proceed North-easterly and activate the next **Waypoint**. Head up the steps to *Gerudo Town*.

## Gerudo Town

Talk with the Gerudo by the steps to start the ***Tornado Ghost*** Side Quest. Choose the *Tornando Echo* from your list to be rewarded with **10 x [Fresh Milk]**.

If you have **400+ Rupees** on you, head into the **Shop** here and purchase the **[Gerudo Sandals]** as they'll stop you to walk on the quicksand in the desert without sinking.

Just bear in mind that they have to be manually put on in the **Equipment Menu**.

Go left and speak with the Gerudo by the steps to start the *Elusive Tumbleweeds* Side Quest.

Immediately go West and climb up the wall here to find the next **[Stamp Stand]**.

02/25 Located!

If you want to complete the *Elusive Tumbleweeds* Side Quest now, drop down, and a lone Tumbleweed should spawn here. Just note its **VERY** sensitive and easy to break!

Very carefully Bind it close to you and slowly take it to the Gerudo to be rewarded with **2 x [Might Crystals]** for your troubles.

018/150 Collected!

If you speak with the Gerudo just above, you can start the *Gerudo Tag Training* Side Quest. We caught her by blocking the whole path with boulders and then running around the opposite way, trapping her, making it super easy!

The reward for catching her is **6 x [Chilly Cactus]**.

Head North now and go inside the main building with the swords above the door to trigger the next part of the Main Quest-line.

Once you're back outside, climb up and over the Gerudo building to the cliffs at the back. You'll find a ladder leading down, go down it.

Use Bind on the new enemy type here and let your best Echo take care of it. Now you can learn the **Platboom Echo***!*

▼ **035/127 Learned!**   ☐

This Echo is very useful as not only does it go up and down (it's a platform after all), but the spikes on the bottom damages any enemies underneath it.

Jump up on the remaining *Platboom* and then drop a *Platboom Echo* on top of the crates to smash them all. Drop down and then use Bind on the giant rock to move it up onto the ledge (using the *Platboom*).

Go right and you can now collect the **[Piece of Heart]** sitting here.

♥ **07/40 Collected?**   ☐

Immediately warp out to the *Oasis Waypoint* and go left to trigger the next part of the Main Quest-line.

Three new Main Quest-lines now appear:

- *Southern Oasis Ruins Rift*
- *Southern Gerudo Desert Rift*
- *Ancestor's Cave of Rest Rift*

Let's start with the first one on the list.

## Main Quest: Southern Oasis Ruins Rift

Head South-east to the map marker and get ready to take out a load of Dark Echoes!

Immediately spawn a *Pot,* then spawn a *Caromadillo Lv. 2.* Jump inside the Pot (to stop the shrieks from freezing you, don't ask us why, it just does!) and clear out all of the enemies with Bind and your Echoes.

Now warp to the *Gerudo Town Waypoint* and head South. *Dohna* asks for a *Cactus Smoothie* for her men. Thankfully, you made just the one they need with the *Business Scrub* earlier on.

What a coincidence!

## Main Quest: Southern Gerudo Desert Rift

Talk to *Dohna* again to give her the drink and this will complete this part of the Main Quest!

Now travel North-east (preferably using your *Caromadillo* Taxi) and by some red pillars is a **[Stamp Stand]**.

*03/25 Located!*

Continue North-east until you see the quicksand. Look North and use some beds as a stepping stone to the **[Piece of Heart]** sitting on the middle stone pillar.

*08/40 Collected?*

From here, travel North-west and climb up the cliff edge until you spot a lone rock on an open area. Lift it up to reveal a **[Might Crystal]** hiding underneath.

*019/150 Collected!*

We're not done yet though. Go South, drop down to the chest by the edge of the Rift and open it for another **[Might Crystal]**!

*020/150 Collected!*

Head down the nearby steps and then use a *Tornando* on the mounds here to destroy them. Now learn both the *Beetle* and the *Beetle-mound Echoes*.

▼ 036/127 Learned! ☐    ▼ 037/127 Learned! ☐

Leave the cave via the way you came in, drop down into the desert, continue Westward and then activate the **Waypoint** here.

Make sure your *Gerudo Sandals* are equipped and head South-east. You'll find the sand shifting, signaling the start of a mini-boss battle. Let's go kick its ass!

##  MINI-BOSS: LANMOLA

### 1st Phase

Not an overly complex fight this one to be honest. If you don't have the **Gerudo Sandals** on, then stand on one of the four solid corners and use **Bind** on its tail to pull it out of the sand and flip it over.

Once its on its back, switch to Swordfighter mode and hack away at it with your sword. Once it flips back over, switch back to regular Zelda and get ready for the second phase.

### 2nd Phase

Head back onto to a solid part (if you don't have the Sandals yet) and wait for the mini-boss to reappear.

Once it does, use **Bind** again on its tail and pull it back onto its back. Switch to Swordfighter mode and hack away and this mini-boss will be a goner.

Once you've collected the rupee stash dropped, you'll also notice that the sandstorm has cleared.

## Main Quest: Ancestor's Cave of Rest Rift

Immediately head North towards the Main Quest marker and head inside the cave.

Use Bind on the rock to move it away from the door, head through, grab the new enemy here with Bind and then use a *Peahat* to get rid of it. You can now learn the **Holmill Echo**.

▼ 038/127 Learned!

Move the rock at the top of the room out of the way, go down the ladder, then use the new Echo on the long patch of sand underneath you. This creates a hole to a chest with a **[Golden Egg]** inside!

Golden Eggs are both worth loads to sell, but they also make the most powerful smoothies possible.

Use another Holmill to drop down and then continue right and up the ladders. Light the unlit fire (however you wish) and you'll complete this main Quest-line.

## En-route Item Pick-ups

It's time to pick up some more useful items and Echoes before we complete the Rift quest here.

Upon exiting the cave, go South-west and look for an opening in-between the cliff faces.

Grab and Bind a *ReDead Echo* to you and hold it in front of the new enemy. It'll freeze and be killed quickly. Very handy.

No go learn the **Club Boarblin Echo**.

▼ 039/127 Learned!

Repeat the same tactic on the **Boomerang Boarblins** a bit further up in the camp. Make sure to learn their Echo too.

▽ **040/127 Learned!** ☐

Climb up the cliff face to the left and head down to the suspicious looking patch of sand on its own. Use a *Holmill* Echo on it to reveal a hidden [Might Crystal].

◆ **021/150 Collected!** ☐

Drop down to the left and go to the top-left corner. A harder enemy will be walking around here. Use your favorite Echo to clear them out so you can learn the **Boomerang Boarblin Lv. 2** and **Club Boarblin Lv. 2 Echoes!**

▽ **041/127 Learned!** ☐

▽ **042/127 Learned!** ☐

Once the chest is unlocked, open it and grab the **[Energy Glove]** inside. Wearing this around Dark Echoes will give you more energy when you defeat Dark Monsters.

Immediately climb up the wall in front of you with a *Crawtula*, then go right and get up to the **[Stamp Stand]** located here.

👤 **04/25 Located!** ☐

Now drop down to the left and enter the nearby cave here.

Inside, quickly drop a Boulder down to stop the Flying Tiles from hitting you. Go up and then drop another Boulder down in front of the square pit. Stand behind it to keep yourself safe.

▼ 043/127 Learned!

Once it's clear, go up through the door, then **immediately** come back into the room and *quickly* learn the **Flying-tile Echo**!

**Top Tip!** *This Echo can actually be stood on and then used to - very quickly - travel across smaller gaps.*

In fact, lets use this trick in the next room! Clear out the *Octorok* and then place a tile down and **quickly** jump on top of it and ride it across the pit.

Do the same at the top (lining up the tile with the blue switch) and it'll hit it, dropping the gates. Use a tile to jump off to the left and open the chest for a **very** handy **100 Rupees!** Wowzers!

Exit the cave then immediately climb up the wall and head North-west.

## Acorn Gathering

There's a man up here who has a mini-game where he'll time you collecting a set number of acorns (that never change location) within a set time limit.

We cover this mini-game in full on page 240, but for this particular version (there's more than one in the game), start with the acorns on the wall at the bottom, and work your way in an anti-clockwise fashion.

You can use the *Flying Tile* as a makeshift platform by the boulders to reach the acorns behind the boulders, and use your *Crawtula* to go up to the acorns higher up.

Beat it in under 1 minute for **20 Rupees**. While you're here, be sure to defeat the ***Mini-Moldorms*** and learn their Echo.

▼ 044/127 Learned!

Go right and drop down into the grassy area where you'll find a new **Waypoint** to activate.

Now warp back to *Gerudo Town* and head into the main *Gerudo* building to continue the Main Quest-line.

### Main Quest: A Rift in the Gerudo Desert

Warp to the *Oasis Waypoint* and immediately use a *Flying Tile* to fly over the nearby pond and try and hit **Tormali**. He'll freak out and reward you with **50 Rupees**, completing *The Flying Tile* Side Quest! It's now time to take on that Rift. Make your way to the yellow marker on the map and enter the Rift!

## STILLED DESERT TEMPLE RUINS

The goal here is to collect **five energy orbs** that are dotted around the map.

## Energy Orb 1

This orb is located West of the starting point. Go up, then left and around the head statue. Use a *Flying Tile* to fly across to the Orb located on top of the pillar.

## Energy Orb 2

From here, head North, up the floating pillar, the proceed right and go down the ladder into the cave.

Use Bind on the *Platbooms* to give you access to the next Orb in the lower-left corner.

Exit the cave then continue northwards.

## Energy Orb 3

Now you can use your *Flying Tiles* or a *Crawtula* to climb up to the top of the sandy area that's on its side. At the top here, use your *Flying Tile* to fly across the gap, lift the **Boulder** and collect the Orb underneath.

## Energy Orb 4

The fourth Orb is found further North on the next sideways piece of land. You can drop down on it from above, or your Tile to fly across to it. Your choice.

## Energy Orb 5

The final Orb is located just over to the left on top of the tree stump. You can use a Trampoline to reach it quickly. Once collected, Tri will give you **2 x [Might Crystals]** as a reward.

023/150 Collected! ■

Once the cut-scenes are over, warp to the Waypoint closest to the Rift and then make your way into the, now open, cave entrance.

# CRYPTIC CAVERN

In the first room, fire a Flying Tile at the switch to open the door. In the next room, use Bind to pull the Wind-cannons down into the abyss in the middle of the room. Head up through the middle door.

In here there's a bunch of new enemies. Use a *Peahat* to clear the nearest one and learn it for the **Pathblade Echo**.

This Echo functions like an even *faster* Taxi outside if you put it in front of you and then Reverse Bond yourself to it! It's awesome!

▼ **045/127 Learned!** ☐

Ignore the other Pathblades, and instead, use a Tile to hit the switch across the gap. Ha!

Before dropping down into the next area, start throwing some *Ignizols* down there as these new enemies are super weak to fire! They'll burn, leaving their **Gibdo Echo** behind.

▼ **046/127 Learned!** ☐

Open the small chest here for a **[Small Key]**. In the next below you, lock-on to the enemies and use your Pathblade Echo to take the enemies out quickly.

Clear out the sand here for **20 Rupees**, before exiting the left-side and then moving the Wind-cannon out of your way. Open the door with the small key.

Head down the ladder and then you can bash the Pathblades down here with your own Pathblades! When you see the chest, you can use Bind on it from below to pull it down to you for the **20 Rupees** inside.

Use your Wind-cannon to clear out the sand in your way, dodge the Pathblades, then use a Tile to fly across the gap to the ladder.

After heading up, go left, up the ladder, step on the switch, go right again, and use an Ignizol on the **Gibdo Lv. 2** (it's basically a ReDead wrapped in bandages).

▼ **047/127 Learned!** ☐

Head right and then use Bind to pull the plug, draining the sand away from in front of this area's main temple.

Immediately warp back outside to the Waypoint by the Rift.

It's time to take on the main dungeon to complete this Main Quest. You ready? Good. Let's go.

Ⓐ Set Pin

Gerudo Sanctum

2F

1F

Ⓐ Set Pin

# DUNGEON: GERUDO SANCTUM

After entering and spotting our dear friend Link, go up the ladder, then go right and drop a Boulder in front of the Wind-cannon. Climb up and around the next cannon, and push the Boulder in front of the next Wind-cannon and go up.

Activate the **Waypoint** here, go in the left room, stand by the door, and drop a Boulder down in front of you. Let the Tiles smash themselves into it and open the chest for **20 Rupees**.

Go right and, in the far-right room, pull down the lever and immediately use a Flying Tile to go right. Jump off and make it through the door before the blocks close.

In the next room, pull the right-hand side to you with Bind and go through. Grab the small key then go back and open the locked door.

In the next room, learn the *Snake-statue Echo*.

▼ 048/127 Learned! ■

In the next room, Bind the flying enemies to you and send out your strongest Echo to take care of them one at a time. Now go learn the *Mothula Echo*.

▼ 049/127 Learned! ■

Head left, then down, and then in the next room, ignore the puzzle completely by using a Flying Tile at the bottom to reach the other side quickly!

Go down the ladder and then use your digging Echo to dig through the sand to the chest containing a **[Golden Egg]**.

Dodge or get rid of the Caromadillo, and then go down the ladder. Activate the **Waypoint** when you get here.

Go right and pull the lower handle to you to spin the door open. In the next room, use a Wind-cannon on the lower sand pile to reveal a chest containing **10 x [Rock Salt]**. Very nice.

Leave this room and go to the far-left room where you'll encounter a new enemy. This enemy can break your Bind on it if you hold it too long, so be quick hitting it with your best Echoes. Once it's gone, collect the *Poe Echo*.

050/127 Learned!

Collect the **[Dungeon Map]** from the chest and then head down through the door.

## Stilled Gerudo Sanctum

We re-appear outside the Stilled version of the area. If you look closely, there's an open window to the right. Make your way inside and claim the hidden room of Rupees. Sweet!

Back outside, go down and left, clearing the path of Dark Echoes along the way, and in the chest in the top-left corner of the sand are **20 Rupees**. Grab them if you want them, then continue heading North-east.

Pull the right-hand handle of the round tower left to re-align the ladder, allowing you to climb up.

Climb to the top and open the chest for **50 Rupees**. Now keep going right, until you're at the top of the temple, and activate the **Waypoint** here.

There's a very easy to miss patch of sand on the left. Use your Holmill here and drop down.

This will cause you to land in a room that you would otherwise keep walking past, wondering how on Earth you get to the chest here! This is how! Open the chest for a cool **50 Rupees**.

Warp back up to the Waypoint in the *Stilled Gerudo Sanctum*, clear out the Dark Echoes, then use a Wind-cannon on the bottom pile of sand to reveal a chest.

Open it to give you your first **[Monster Stone]**. You can trade these in with a specific character later on in the game.

Now go up to the North-eastern corner of the Temple and use a Flying Tile to cross the gap to the North-east. Clear the sand and then pull the **left-hand** handle to the right to re-align the ladder.

Climb up and learn the - important for this dungeon - *Hawk Statue Echo*.

▼ 051/127 Learned! ◻

Warp back to the Temple's Stilled Waypoint and then drop down the bottom-right side of the Temple, and enter the door down here.

## Gerudo Sanctum

After pulling the lever all the way back (use Bind to allow you to get further away), go right, jump across the to right-hand platforms, and then use a Tile to cross to the other side before the exit shuts.

Once in the next room, quickly approach the red statues to learn the *Cat-statue Echo*.

Watch out for the ReDead in here and use your strongest Fire Echoes to clear the room. Move the Cat Statue at the top out of the way, then activate the **Waypoint**. Get your *Peahat* ready and enter the door for a fight…

## BOSS FIGHT: DARK LINK (BOW)

### 1st Phase

Right at the start chase after Dark Link and use **Bind** on him to lift him into the air.

Drag him into the middle of the arena and press **Y** (while still holding X) to bring out your Echo.

Drag Dark Link into your Echo's many super pointy spikes to deal loads of damage to him. After three hits, it's time for Phase Two!

### 2nd Phase

It's time for a 3-vs-1 showdown! Switch to Swordfighter mode and let's hunt down the first Dark Link!

Jump over the green blocks if they're in your way. Three clean hits from your sword will take it down!

Pick up the second Dark Link with **Bind** and drop it down the hole (it makes fighting the other Dark Link easier as the Dark Link you just dropped takes a bit of time to get back into the fight).

Three sword hits on each Dark Link is all that it takes to send them back to where they came from. Nice one, you've got yourself the **[Bow]**!

As is tradition in all Zelda games, it's time to use your new weapon as soon as you get it!

Go through the door and then use your newfound Bow to take out the Beetle Mound and the Dark Web across the gap. Switch back to regular Zelda, and use a Tile to cross the gap to the ladder.

Go up, activate the **Waypoint** here, and then use your Bind ability on the handle of the flamethrower located *directly above you*, You can pull this so it turns to face away, and then use a Crawtula to climb up, allowing you to simply walk over to the chest!

Drop down into the caged area, and then learn the *Elephant-statue Echo*.

Open the chest for a **[Small Key]** then leave the way you came.

Warp back to the Waypoint where the gold plaque is by the closed door, and then drop an **Elephant-statue Echo** and a **Hawk-statue Echo** on the red blocks to unlock the door ahead!

(This saves you going into every room to read the hint in the slab as the solution to this puzzle **doesn't change**).

Head through the door, pull the plug (draining the sand), head into the next room and then let's solve the dungeon's Big Key puzzle!

## Big Key Puzzle

Alright, the simple solution is as follows:

1. Turn the small wheel **left three times**.
2. Turn the small wheel **left one more time**.
3. Grab the blue handle with Bind and **pull it right once**.

That's all there is to it! Grab the **[Big Key]** from the chest. Make your way up to the stairs and activate the **Waypoint** here!

Make sure your health is full and you're ready to take on this boss!

## 1st Phase

Make sure you've got an Echo (like a *Boulder*) set to **Y** and then your first goal is to dodge the sand waves the boss fires at you.

The easiest way to do that is to stand behind one of the statues in the corner of the room.

Once the boss goes underground, run into the middle of the room and drop a *Boulder* down so that it's directly between you and the boss.

The boss will smash into it, giving you *loads* of time. Switch to Swordfighter mode and get as many hits in as you can. You need to repeat this process one more time to start phase two.

028/150 Collected! ■

## 2nd Phase

Once the sand level drops, if you don't have the **Gerudo Sandals** on, then we recommend you stay around the bottom of the screen to avoid the sand tornadoes.

Use a *Boulder* to stop the sand waves (which are faster), and keep an eye out for the shadow when the boss tries to land on you from above!

Finally, use another *Boulder* to stop the boss when it charges at you and hack away in Swordfighter form to end this battle victoriously and get **5 x [Might Crystals]**.

# THE JABUL WATERS RIFT

## Water Way to Save Everyone

With the Gerudo people saved, let's take a useful pit stop at Lueberry's house. Warp to the Waypoint by his home then, for every **10 Might Crystals** you've found, you can upgrade your Sword, Bow, or Energy Bar.

If you've been following our guide closely, then you should have over 20. If so, we recommend upgrading your **Sword** and **Energy Bar**.

## Echo and Item Sweep

As soon as you leave Lueberry's house, take a right, go up the ramp, use your tiles to get on top of the trees, go North-east, go a little bit right, and then go into the cave. Go to the top of the cave, pull the chest out, and inside is a **[Golden Egg]**.

Leave the cave, get back on top of the trees, go above the cave, take a right, until you see the next **[Stamp Stand]**.

Once you're finished, go up and left. towards the edge of the lake and then go across to the West.

05/25 Located!

Jump into the water and you will see, if you pay very close attention, a very large boulder at the bottom of the lake.

Use bind to lift the boulder up out of the water and underneath is a **[Might Crystal]**. Swim back out and go up northwest to the middle of the lake and you will see a rift.

029/150 Collected!

# STILLED LAKE HYLIA

You can now go inside this and you will enter Stilled Lake Hylia. Now in here, we suggest you use your Flying Tile to go across the water and you need to get three energy orbs to clear this Rift.

## Energy Orb 1

If you want to get rid of all the dark echo fish, we strongly suggest that you use your bind to pull them out of the water and then drop them down into the rift, making it safe to jump into the water and get the energy orb.

## Energy Orb 3

Use your tiles to fly between each of the rift parts and you can jump in and out of the water as and when required to stop you from falling.

Now swim to the top left corner of the rift and swim under the trees. You won't really see the opening but it's there, trust us.

## Energy Orb 2

Once you've got the energy orb, go northeast, start swimming up, pulling any enemies off, dropping them into the rift, and then you need to make your way to the top North-eastern corner where you'll see a boulder in the water with some cliff edges.

Pull the boulder out of the way and in there you can grab the second energy orb.

Move the final boulder out of the way to grab the third and final energy orb. This will upgrade Tri's energy. You'll also get **2 x** [Might Crystals] as a reward.

**031/150 Collected!**

Once you've finished, exit the rift and it's now time to go north east across the river.

Make your way to the middle of *Lake Hylia* and there should be a **Waypoint** outside a cave. Activate it, then head inside.

This is where the **Great Fairy** resides. Now, don't forget, if you ever need any fairies there's always two fairies in here that can go in your bottles.

Approach the top and chat to the great fairy and pay to upgrade *at least* one accessory slot.

If you have 400 rupees or more, then you can upgrade two accessory slots. Otherwise, you should have enough rupees to upgrade the first slot to two.

Exit the cave, and this time make your way North-east again.

Now once you reach the very north of the lake, you should be in *Hyrule Field*.

Look very closely by the edge of the water, where there's a big tree and there's a boulder in the

bottom right corner of the tree. Move the boulder and pick up the [Might Crystal] from underneath the boulder.

032/150 Collected!

Continue west, just a little bit, past the wooden sign. and you'll see another boulder in between two trees also by the water. Move this boulder for another [Might Crystal].

033/150 Collected!

Go back to the right, past the Zelda poster, go north at the sign and take a look up to the northeast where you'll see a lot of rocks up on a little cliff edge.

Get onto the tree, look for a single gray boulder all by itself, lift it up and grab the [Might Crystal] from underneath.

034/150 Collected!

Jump off to the left and activate the next **Waypoint**. nearby. You will now be in *Eastern Hyrule Field*.

Continue North and if you pay close attention you should see the next **[Stamp Stand]**.

Once you've got it, go up the stairs, head north and clear out this encampment. You will also find your next echo here, which will be a *Spear Moblin Lv. 2*.

Inside the chest, you'll find 7 x **[Radiant Butter]**.

Make your way out and head to the right. Clear out the Moblin that's here for your next Echo. Which will be a *Sword Moblin Echo.*

Continue up the two sets of steps and you will now trigger your next Side Quest *Let's Play a Game* if you speak to the guy outside the building.

This is technically a dungeon with a mini boss at the end. So, let's get to it!

In the first room, you want to use arrows on the green ball Echoes known as **Sparks**.

▼ 056/127 Learned! □

Now, what you're *supposed* to do is encourage them to go into the yellow square boxes in each room (opening the door).

However, you can just use the Spark Echo instead! So, fire the sparks **directly into the boxes**, bypassing a lot of the puzzles in this dungeon!

For the first box, use **three** Sparks Echoes. Go into the next room, jump up and fire **two Spark Echoes** to open both doors.

Head to the right and go to the bottom, bottom corner and immediately fire two forwards (stand by the fence) to open up the chest, to reveal the chest. And inside the chest is **50 Rupees**. Exit and go to the left.

Pull the chest to you with Bind and open it for 5 x **[Rock Salt]**.

Now you can use your arrows to clear out the spark echoes, to clear the sparks. And go to the right, head to the water, swim down, open the chest for **50 Rupees** in the water.

Now, swim up, jump onto the wooden crates, head down the ladder. In the next room, select the boulder and you're now in the boss's room. Let's take a look at how to beat him.

## 1st Phase

For phase one, focus on re-directing the path of the boss using *Boulders* so that you pin it down to one part of the room (we chose the middle as it'll get there by itself quite quickly, but any corner also works well).

Keep in mind that you can make it change direction immediately by using **Bind** on it once (this allows you to "bring it back to you").

Once it's trapped, use *Bombfish/Pathblades* to start Phase two.

## 2nd Phase

The goal here is to use *Boulders* to direct the Mini-Smogs to each other so they reform into the main boss again.

Look at how they're traveling, anticipate where they're going, and use *Boulders* to guide them to a corner of the room. Hit them with **Bind** to change their direction.

The goal is to use the same *Boulder + Bombfish (or Pathblade)* combo to take him to the final phase.

## 3rd Phase

The boss now splits in **five** smaller versions. Once again, you need to use a series of well-placed *Boulders* to lead each cloud to each other.

Focus on luring them into the same corner (use your *Boulders* to block off one of the corners) and quickly guide them to where you need them to go.

Once again, block the large boss in and *Bombfish* it back to where it came from. Nice one!

Make sure to collect your [Piece of Heart] that was dropped by the boss before leaving.

09/40 Collected? ■

Head back outside, speak to *Sago*, completing the Side Quest and you're given the [Ancient Charm] accessory as thanks. This is good to use because it reduces the damage you take.

Once you're finished, exit to the South east and very close to where you were standing, there's going to be another lone gray rock sitting on a little green patch of grass on a cliff. Lift up the rock and underneath is a [Might Crystal].

035/150 Collected! ■

Drop down, keep heading to the south east, start jumping on some trees and make your way back towards *Lake Hylia*.

Go South-west and near the edge of the water is a cave. Head inside the cave clear out the blue Zols here, learn it and you will now have the **Hydrozol Echo**.

▽ 057/127 Learned! ■

It's interesting to note that these echoes get bigger if you expose them to water such as puddles or rain.

Now, in the next room, swim under the water, head up the ladder and when you reappear, what you're supposed to do is use the Hydrozol to put out all of the fires to make sure that **none of the lanterns are lit.**

So, lift the Hydrozol with Bind and move it around the room putting out **all** the fires. With all the fires out, head up and you will get a [Piece of Heart].

10/40 Collected? ■

Exit, go to the left, continue left again and exit the cave.

From here, go North-east into the water, then go up and left a bit when you hit the sandy shore.

You should see a little crab creature in the water on your left. Hold it with Bind, let your Echo damage it, and you will have a new Echo. The **Sand Crab Echo**.

▼ 058/127 Learned!

Go back to the new **Waypoint** that's nearby, and you will now be in a new area, **Jabul Waters**.

We now begin the main quest, the **Jabul Waters Rift**. As soon as you finish talking to the people Pick up the next **[Stamp Stand]**.

07/25 Located!

Now you can have a chat with the people here. Firstly though, jump down into the water and swim underneath the wooden pier that faces South for a **[Might Crystal]** hidden in the water.

036 /150 Collected!

However, if you speak to the lady on the dock with the red exclamation mark, you will begin a new side quest where you have to take the fish to your son.

This is the *Deliver the Grilled Fish* Side Quest. First thing you should do is learn the echo of the fish, teaching you the **Grilled Fish Echo**.

▼ 059/127 Learned!

It is important to note though that for this particular side quest, the echo version of the grilled fish **does not work**.

It has to be the one that the mum gives you. You can't cheat this one we're afraid. So, we suggest that you grab it with bind and lift it all the way North.

The goal here is to find her son who is North of her position. You'll know you're on the right track because you'll see a broken stone pillar crossing over the water.

Be careful though, because you're going to see some Moblins, so we suggest that you get up onto the nearby trees and use a Flying Tile to reach her son, *Anub*, and give him the fish.

While you're here, drop down, clear out all the enemies and in the chest you will find 10 x **[Riverhorses]**.

Go North past the son. By using the trees. And we suggest that you go Westward. You will now find you're going near lots of water.

Not too far from the corner of the Rift there's a tree on its own square patch of land with some purple flowers and a patch of sand. beside it, Use your Holmill Echo here to dig up a [Might Crystal].

037/150 Collected!

Head back to the son and then go North into the *Zora River*. Activate the **[Stamp Stand]** near the Rift.

08/25 Located!

Now head East towards the map marker and then activate the **Waypoint** just off to the right, now head inside *Lord Jabu-Jabu's Den* to progress the Main Quest.

Exit the den, then go left, around the outskirts of the Rift, and head North into the cave near the waterfall/Rift edge.

Throw the boulder by the water's edge at the new enemy in the water and learn the *Bombfish Echo*!

060/127 Learned!

This Echo is a bomb (on a timer) that doesn't *have* to be used in the water. Which means, you now effectively have access to bombs, allowing you to blow up those weak rocks dotted around the world! Kaboom!

Head right, use your new Bombfish on the Sea Urchins in the water, and also on the new fish enemy-type. Kill one and learn the *Tangler Echo*.

Head down the nearby ladder and then use a Bombfish on the cracked block at the bottom of the cave. If you find that the Bombfish *doesn't* start flashing red, then using Bind works, while allowing you to move it into position.

Make it through the watery tunnel, stopping for air at the bubbles dotted around if needed, then in the next room, clear it of all Bombfish to open the doors.

After jumping out of the water, lift up a Brazier so it sets the wood under the chest on fire. Open the chest for a handy **[Golden Egg]**.

Climb up the ladders, hit the switch, then go back outside.

Continue up North from the cave's entrance to find *another* cave by a waterfall, head inside.

This cave is a series of Bind movement puzzles. For the first room, jump onto the crate moving around the water, then use Bind on the crate behind the fence and let go of it when it's over the switch.

Repeat this for the next room, however, you *have to jump up while still using Bind* to lift the crate into the air. You need to do this **four times** (while the crate you're on is still moving), to reach the switch with the crate.

For the final room, do an **Extended Bind** (by holding **Y**) so that the crate appears at the back of the room. Immediately Bind it, then jump up and back to hit the switch, revealing a chest. Open the chest for a cool **100 Rupees!**

After exiting the cave, head West and activate the **Waypoint** right outside *River Zora Village*.

Go up, enter the shop and, hopefully you should have a *lot* more than the 350 Rupees needed to buy the **[Zora's Flippers]**.

Head East (up the ramp), then go right, swim down in the water, and open the chest for **20 Rupees**.

Head West and then up until you see the hut with the red cloth on top and Braziers outside.

## The Jabul Water's Rift

After speaking with the chief, warp back to the *Seesyde Village Waypoint*. Look up and blow up the cracked wall with a Bombfish for a chest containing 20 Rupees.

Head back down to the mother whose son you gave the fish to and she'll reward you with 10 x **[Bubble Kelp]** for your time.

Go North-east to *Crossflows Plaza* and speak with *Dradd* here to move the story forwards. Go down and activate the Waypoint here.

Head right and speak with the *Business Scrub* to start (and finish) the *Out of Bubble Kelp* Side Quest!

Immediately go South-east into the open water and use Bind to grab the white bird flying around. Drag it under the water and then learn the **Albatrawl Echo**.

▼ **062/127 Learned!** ☐

> **Top Tip!** *We can't believe we're even writing this in a guide for a Nintendo game but... it's actually **really** effective to **drown** enemies as most of the non-water based enemies can't swim! We never thought we'd see that as a viable strategy but, it is!*

Now dive underwater and look for the circle of seaweed. Spin dash into the middle seaweed to reveal a hidden **[Might Crystal]**.

💎 **038/150 Collected!** ☐

Swim West from here, past the small island, then pull up the chest from the waterbed and open it for **50 Rupees**.

Swim South and look for a large cracked rock in the water. Blow it open with a Bombfish and collect the hidden [Might Crystal].

💎 **039/150 Collected!** ☐

From here, travel East and then activate the **Waypoint** on the island with the fish statue in the middle. Swim down and into the underwater entrance to arrive in the *Sea Zora Village*.

Head up to the throne room and then warp to *Crossflows Plaza* as soon as you can.

Go up to trigger a scene that pushes the Main Quest forwards. Once you regain control of Zelda, warp to the Jabu-Jabu waypoint and then go South-east to see the Acorn mini-game man again.

For the strategies on beating this version of the mini-game, please head to page 240.

After finishing the mini-game, dive into the water and drown the blue jumping enemy here for the *Tektite Echo*.

▼ **063/127 Learned!** ☐

Immediately warp to the *River Zora Village* waypoint to trigger a new Main Quest…

## Chaos at River Zora Village

Proceed Northwards and go through through the gap in the cliff (behind the huts), head right and get ready to enter the Rift!

# STILLED UPPER ZORA RIVER

There's a total of **five** energy orbs to find here. So, let's get to it.

## Energy Orb 1

Head south (down the broken pillars), turn right, then use a Flying Tile to reach the pillar with the Energy Orb on it.

## Energy Orb 2

Swim up the water, go North-east, up onto the tree, then down into the cave. Swim down to the bottom (using the Bombfish to blow up the blocks) and in the bottom-left is the next Energy Orb.

## Energy Orb 3

Swim left and then use a Bombfish on the jellyfish enemy. Be sure to learn it, for the *Biri Echo*.

▼ 064/127 Learned! ☐

Exit the water, then dispatch the Dark Echo up here to reveal the third Energy Orb.

## Energy Orb 4

Exit the cave, then proceed Westward. If you use Flying Tiles, you can reach the Energy Orb sitting on top of the ground that's sitting sideways.

## Energy Orb 5

The final Energy Orb can be found to the left and down in a small pool of water. A quick Tile ride over to it will work. Tri will reward you with **2 x** [Might Crystals].

041/150 Collected! ☐

## The Jabul Waters Rift

With the last Main Quest-line completed, immediately drop down to the left and speak with the child Zora to start the Side Quest *The Zora Child's Fate*.

You can finish this one now by going into the nearby hut and dropping the following Echoes into the pool of water in front of her:

1. Tangler
2. Bombfish
3. Biri

She'll now give you the - *very useful* - **[Zora's Scale]**. This allows you to stay underwater for a *lot* longer!

Now use a Crawtula to climb directly North until you see a square pool of water with a Fairy floating around. Dive under the water here to collect a [Piece of Heart].

**11/40 Collected?**

Now head directly West, drop down and by the Rift is a new, flying enemy. Kill one with your Bow and go learn the *Needlefly Echo*.

**065/127 Learned!**

Walk South-west from here and you'll soon spot the next **[Stamp Stand]**.

**09/25 Located!**

From here, drop down past the trees, then use a Bombfish on the cracked wall to reveal a chest. Inside you'll find the **[Silver Brooch]**.

Continue Southwards until you spot the Moblin camp. Clear them all out and be sure to open the chest for a super handy **3 x [Might Crystals]**. Sweet!

Warp to the Waypoint for the *Zora Sea Village* (near *Zora Cove*), swim down to the trees, hang a left, then remove the Sea Urchins surrounding the chest. Open it for a cool **20 Rupees**.

Swim directly to the right until you reach another chest. This one contains **5 x [Bubble Kelp]**.

Continue swimming to the right and look for the Biri and Sea Urchin near a large, cracked stone in the water. Bomb this to reveal a **[Piece of Heart]**.

While you're here, swim North-east for the next **[Stamp Stand]**.

## Rampage in Zora Cove

Head North to trigger the next Main Quest-line. After speaking with *Dradd,* swim down into the cave entrance right below you.

With the Zora's Scale equipped, swim down into the cave and spin dash into the crystals to light them up.

Be sure to get rid of the fish in here, as they're the stronger version of the Tangler. Learn the **Tangler Lv. 2 Echo** before you swim up and out of the water.

Once the cut-scene has finished, warp out to *Jabu-Jabu's Den* (just North of *Crossflow Plaza.*

Head into the Den and then your goal is to reconstruct the broken stand. Remove the blue bit of rock, then use Bind on the nearby smaller bit to lock it in. The last piece can be brought out of the water below you.

## 1st Phase

Start by selecting the *Bombfish* Echo and then proceed to swim underwater (which is easier than trying to jump around all the debris at the top). If you've unlocked the **Zora Scale**, then you can stay here for *ages*.

Once the boss starts inhaling, drop a *Bombfish* and then swim away! Once the bomb explodes in its mouth, quickly swim back in, get up beside it, and use your Swordfighter mode to hit it hard!

## 2nd Phase

To be honest, the remaining two phases are pretty much a repeat of the first one.

Granted, it'll chuck out more enemies each time, but if you're swimming around underwater, you're *much* less likely to be hit.

If you're getting hit more than you'd like, you can always drop an *Old Bed* on the water and rest in it briefly to top up your health.

Otherwise, it's not too difficult a battle, so don't stress. You've got this.

# STILLED JABUL WATERS

This Rift will take you to the second major dungeon so far. So, let's get to it!

Once you enter the Rift, go North, then West, swim through the water, step out onto the central pillar, then use a Tile to reach the trees on the right.

Keep swimming up and proceeding North until you see two square blocks on their own (with gaps in the middle). You can learn the **Water Block Echo** here.

▼    067/127 Learned!    □

> **Top Tip!** *To create a pillar of water you can just swim straight up, stand still and keep pressing* **Y***. The Water blocks will stack on top of each other!*
>
> *You can also place a Water block on the ground and use Bind to drag in any enemy that can't swim, to basically drown it on the spot! Yes, it's cruel, but also* **very** *effective!*

Continue North-east until you see the wall of broken water blocks. You can save a ton of time and skip it by using a Crawtula to climb up the left-hand wall, straight to the top! Ha!

Save time by using Flying Tiles to quickly fly between the little water islands, (jumping in and out of the water as needed).

When your reach the jellyfish, swim right, get out, then fly across to the right. Climb up the boats and open the chest here for **10 x Riverhorses**.

Make your way West, swimming carefully past the enemies, then on the far left is a chest containing **50 Rupees**.

Go right, then up the Jabu-Jabu, to the dungeon's entrance…

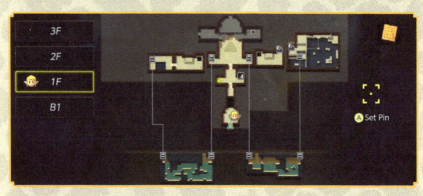

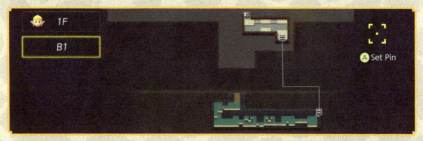

Alright, believe it or not, this dungeon can either be long (with a few new Echoes and some decent Rupees to be had), or... you can go and skip about 90% of the dungeon!

While we'll give you the full solution (because of the Echoes and Rupees on offer for doing so), here's the abbreviated super-quick path for reaching the boss:

## Super-Quick Method!

1. Use a *Tile* or a few *Beds* in the first room to skip the floor breaking.
2. DO NOT press the water button. Instead, use a *Crawtula* to crawl up the right-hand wall to the second floor.
3. Go right and collect the **Big Key** ASAP.
4. Use the Crawtula to climb straight up to the Boss' door!

It's literally *that simple*!

## The "intended" Method

Alright, be sure to activate the **Waypoint** in the entrance. Then, when you reach the next room, **please** use a Flying Tile to reach the next door. Falling down does absolutely nothing but waste your time! (Trust us on this one).

Activate the next **Waypoint** n this room and then stand on the **Pink** button to initiate the water.

## Blue Water Grate

Head down the ladder on the left, then make sure your Zora's Scale and Flippers are equipped.

Dive in, then hit the crystals, and use a Bombfish on the new Deku enemy waiting for you in the dark. Be sure to learn the **Bio Deku Baba Echo**.

▼ **068/127 Learned!** ■

Swim to the bottom and go right for a chest in the dark which has **100 Rupees** in it! Sweet! Swim up and left and leave the water via the ladder.

In the next room is a cheeky little puzzle. The goal is to light all of the lanterns. However, one is at the bottom of the pool of water. The solution is to use Bind to bring it up to the top and then light it, opening the door.

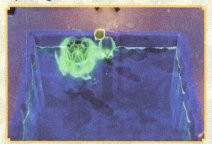

Step on the **Blue Switch** in the next room, drop down, climb up the ladder, then head for the ladder on the far right.

## Red Water Grate

Leave the ladder, then use your Flying Tile to zip past both sets of water and open the chest for the **[Dungeon Map]**.

Drop down into the water, swim up to the ladder, then you'll be in the main puzzle room.

Use your Bombfish *through the fence* to take out the two sharks here. Then, lock-on to the Octorok and use a Peahat on it to kill it.

Drop down into the water, swim *under* the fence (through the gap you can't really see), then grab the *Chompfin Echo*.

▼ *069/127 Learned!*  ☐

Clear out the remaining Octoroks on the pillars using Arrows and then use Bind on the box that's blocking the underwater hole in the grating.

Grab the **50 Rupees** from the chest on the left, go right, then use a Tile to skip the tightrope part and jump off through the gap on the left.

Clear the next room that's full of crabs, go through the door, and step on the **Red Switch** to raise the water level even higher. Exit this area, then ride the water jet up and head left.

## Yellow Water Grate

The next room is full of rushing water, logs, and enemies. Skip all this nonsense by using Flying Tiles to reach the stationary platforms (bottom-center of the room, then left-hand wall), then the exit.

In this room there's five switches to hit to open the door. The quickest way to hit the central and right-hand ones are with arrows.

Spin into the underwater one to activate it, then use a Peahat on the far left-hand switch.

Jump out of the water, then pull the closest crates off and then use a Caromadillo to smash through the row of boxes and hit the final switch quickly.

Head through the door and in the next room, you can either use Bind to drown the Tektites in here, or Swordfighter mode, it's up to you.

Go through the door and step on the **Yellow Switch**. Drop down, then proceed right to the final ladder.

## Green Water Grate

As soon as you drop into the water, use Bind on the boulder and move the wooden plank away. Swim down and open the chest here for a sweet **[Golden Egg]**.

Swim back up, then right, and continue down using Bind to remove the Boulders and wooden planks in the way. Use a Bombfish on the cracked block, swim down, and open the big chest for the **[Big Key]**!

Swim back up, then right, and use more Bombfish (or Bind) to remove the row of wooden crates in your way. Swim up.

In the next room, switch to Swordfighter mode and lock-on to each enemy and use Arrows to clear the room as safely as possible.

In the next room, clear the Dekus, then use Bind on a Pot in the corner of the room and drop it on the Green Switch to raise the water high enough to reach the dungeon's boss!

Drop down, use Bind on the huge boulder and wood to clear the way.

Now ride the water all the way up to the boss door. Thankfully, it's a **super** easy battle - with the right strategy of course...

## 1st Phase

Immediately upon gaining control of Zelda, swim to the top of the boss and swap to *Swordfighter* mode. You can clear all of the top of the boss away in one swipe!

Once it's on its back, hack away and then swim away as it spins around. Once the scale re-grow, go back in for a second go and repeat.

## 2nd Phase

The second phase can be finished quickly by swimming across and up to the far-right side of the water, switching to *Swordfighter* mode again and then dropping down on

it's head, swiping while you do so. This will drop it on its back, allowing you to hack away and kick-off the third, and final, phase.

## 3rd Phase

The final phase can be over with super quickly as well. Simply wait underneath the platform and the boss will come down and swim under you.

Another round of *Swordfighter* form will send this boss off to a watery grave.

# STILL MISSING

## We're far from being done yet...

That was quite a haul you've ended up with. Not only has Tri given you another **5 x [Might Crystals]**, but you've got another Heart Container, *and* some Echoes cost one less shard to cast! Sweet!

052/150 Collected!

Warp to Jabu-Jabu's Den and then go up and right, use the Water echo to reach the [Piece of Heart] on top of the pillar.

049/150 Collected!

Tri's power has increased!

13/40 Collected?

Before we move on, let's grab a few more useful items first. Warp to *River Zora Village* then make your way Eastward until you come to the Moblin group in the water.

Clear them out and claim the **[Golden Egg]** from the chest. Now go down and left to the chest in the water for **3 x [Might Crystals]**. Very nice.

Now warp to Lueberry's house and upgrade your Bow (as you can't upgrade anything else - yet).

Once you're ready, it's time to head out and do a few more things before we progress the Main Quest-line.

Leave Luberry's house and travel North-west until you reach the guy stuck in between the two cliff faces.

Use Bind to move the rocks and boxes before chatting to him to automatically complete the **The Blocked Road** Side Quest!

Go up and activate the nearby **Waypoint**. Travel in a North-easterly direction and be sure to take out one of the flying *Guay* Birds and learn its Echo.

▼ *070/127 Learned!* □

There's also a chest nearby in the ground. Pull it out and open it for **5 x [Floral Nectar]**.

From here, travel North-west and pick up the lone Boulder surrounded by grass for a [Might Crystal].

💎 *053/150 Collected!* ☐

Travel North towards *Hyrule Castle* and activate the **Waypoint** here.

## Save Hyrule Town

With that dramatic scene out of the way, it's time to kick some butt! Switch to Swordfighter mode and dispatch all of the Dark Echoes quickly (use your upgraded Bow on the Keese).

Head right for a cut-scene, then go into the far-left house for another Now go up and jump into the well. Step into the Rift that Tri makes for you and then head outside to appear in the Stilled version of *Hyrule Castle Town*.

# STILLED HYRULE CASTLE TOWN

As soon as you arrive in the Stilled version, jump on top of the house and use a Flying Tile to travel directly North.

Drop down by the water feature, then hang a right by the fallen tower, fly across the gap to the right, and you can use Bind on the chest up above you to bring it closer for **5 x [Monster Fangs]**.

Head left back towards the water feature and go up. Pull the chest out of the ground and open it for **7 x [Radiant Butter]**. Activate the **Waypoint** while you're here.

From here, use the Water block to create a tower you can swim up and jump onto the broken castle wall. Fly across for a chest with **20 Rupees** inside.

Fly back to the Waypoint, then swim up the wall in front of you. Go right, then swim up the next wall, and carefully jump between the small pools of water.

This leads you to the *Stilled version of Hyrule Castle*. You've got this.

## Stilled Hyrule Castle

Activate the **Waypoint**, head upstairs, then use your Swordfighter form to take out the *Darknut Lv. 2* guard.

▼ **071/127 Learned!** ☐

Head into the next room and use Bind on the chair to move it, revealing a ladder down.

Continue on and you'll soon appear in *Hyrule Castle - Dungeon Edition*! Oh, and switch your accessories to the *Ancient Charm* (reduced damage) and the *Energy Glove* (extra Dark Energy).

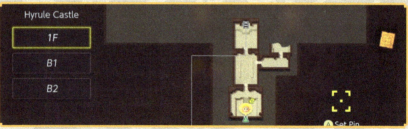

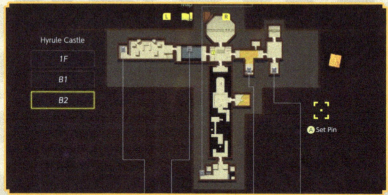

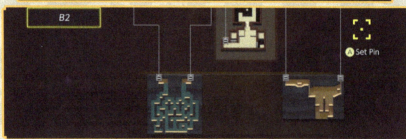

# DUNGEON: HYRULE CASTLE

Activate the **Waypoint** before pulling open the wall with Bind. You can quickly sneak past all of the Dark Guards by waiting for them to turn and look away.

It's also worth having your Water Echo ready as you can quickly use it to reach the upper levels where the guards can't see you.

If a guard spots you, block them in with some Boulders and then get up high again to stay clear.

In the next room, read the diary and then activate the **Waypoint**.

In the next room, let your Darknut Lv. 2 Echo deal with the other Darknuts wandering around.

Keep going left, quickly open the chest for a **[Monster Stone]**, head right and down for two more chests.

One contains **5 x [Floral Nectar]** and the other **3 x [Twisted Pumpkins]**.

Switch to Swordfighter mode if the Dark blobs catch you, it's the quickest way to deal with the Echoes.

Continue down and in the next room, clear out the Dark Keese before using an Extended Bind to send a *Brazier Echo* across the gap, lighting the torch.

For the far-right torch, spawn a Brazier on the platform and then use Bind to move it up to the unlit torch.

Light the last two torches and go through the door. In the next room, use your Arrows to kill the enemy up ahead, walk around then jump down to learn the *Gustmaster Echo*.

072/127 Learned!

Go up and then grab the next Gustmaster in a Bind, and drag it off into the abyss.

Fly across the gap, then clear Ignizols out and in the room on the right, blow away the sand to reveal a chest with the **[Dungeon Map]** in it.

Back in the previous room, use a Gustmaster on the Dark Zols to blow them off, then fly across to the door at the top of the room.

Activate the **Waypoint** in this room, head left, fly across to the ladder opposite and go down.

Swap your damage accessory for your Zora's Scale (for now), and then swim down and to the left for a chest with **20 Rupees**.

> *Top Tip! If you get lost in here, just look at your map as the whole layout is revealed on-screen for you!*

Keep swimming down and left (using your Swordfighter form on the dark webs) and there's a chest right at the bottom with a handy **100 Rupees** in it!

Now swim up and to the left, climbing the ladder out. Switch your Accessory back from the *Zora's Scale* to the *Ancient Charm* again.

In this room, use a water column to get up high quickly, then use a Tile to fly between the columns, allowing you to reach the switch.

Carefully drop down to the chest from behind and open it for the **[Small Key]**.

Fly across to the door on the right, in the next room, fly across to the other side, then go right past the Waypoint.

In the next room, clear out the enemies, then drop the Boulders up by the - easy to miss - crack in the wall. Drop a Bombfish on it and head through the gap for a chest with **50 Rupees** inside.

Go South and then open the locked door with the small key.

Dash past the first Gustmaster, and then time your Tile to fly over the next one to the other side.

In this room, either drown the Darknuts, or use your Swordfighter form, your choice.

Make sure to learn the **Ball-and-Chain Echo** as it's *amazing*!

 073/127 Learned!

**Top Tip!** *If you Bind this Echo and move it around a room, it'll deal* **serious** *damage* **and** *the ball and chain offers a very impressive reach for those further away enemies!*

In the next room, open the three chests to reveal a **[Golden Egg]**, **[Frog Ring]** and the **[Big Key]**.

The Frog Ring basically allows you to jump as high as your Swordfighter form does.

Now go back to the left and open up the door to the Dungeon's Boss! We wonder who it is?...

## Boss Fight: Ganon (again)

### 1st Phase

Just like in the original battle, move out of the way of the lunges, switch to Swordfighter mode, and attack Ganon (two lunges should do if you're quick enough).

### 2nd Phase

For phase two, you should jump over the spinning trident and then go straight to Ganon as he's frozen there until the trident returns. Get in as many hits as you can.

Once you see Ganon spin his trident in front of him, drop a *Boulder* down and this not only stops the *Fire Keese*, but they'll drop refills for your *Swordfighter* energy bar! Sweet!

If you're feeling brave, you can also nip from behind the boulder with a charged **Bow** shot for some extra damage.

## 3rd Phase

For phase three, Ganon will bust out his trusty energy ball for another game of ping pong. Be sure to hit it back to him enough times to force him to change his attack.

Bear in mind he'll also use the previous two attack patterns as well, so pay attention!

## 4th Phase

Finally, this is every previous attack, just sped up. You've got this!

Once you defeat Dark Ganon, you'll likely earn enough energy to upgrade Tri to Level 5, reducing the cost of even more Echoes, along with a further **5 x [Might Crystals]**!

058/150 Collected!

# LANDS OF THE GODDESSES

## Mountainous Perils Await...

Once all of the cut-scenes end and you have control of Zelda again, be sure to learn the **Zelda's Bed Echo**. This bed is the best one for laying in to recover energy quickly.

▼ 074/127 Learned! ■

### Rescuing the Hero Link

Leave the castle, then go the top of the castle where a right-hand corner of the castle (by the water) to find a [Piece of Heart]. Nice!

♥ 14/40 Collected? ■

Jump onto the central roof of the castle where a [Might Crystal] is hiding in plain sight! Cheeky!

059/150 Collected! ■

Jump down into the middle of Hyrule Town and look for the bird weather vane. In classic Zelda fashion, there's something under it! Use Bind to move it to the side and head down the ladder.

Open the chest down here for **2 x [Might Crystals]**!

061/150 Collected! ■

Now head into the Town's shop and purchase the **[Stone Anklet]** for 400 Rupees.

Go to the castle entrance and speak with *Beecher* to start the *One Soldier too Many* Side Quest.

For now, run South-west, jump across the castle moat, towards some trees, then hidden under a lone bush (in the middle of the trees) is a [Might Crystal].

*062/150 Collected!*

Head North towards the West-side of the castle and speak with the Acorn man to start his Acorn-gathering mini-game.

If you can collect them all in under 17-seconds (see page 240 for our full guide to all mini-games), you'll earn **3 x [Might Crystals]**.

*065/150 Collected!*

Now use a water column to get up onto the castle walkway and speak with the guard up here. Drop down and talk to the guard by the well.

Now talk to the guard inside the guardhouse just above you and ask about "Missing Equipment."

Tell them that you know it's an Echo and that you know who it is "Near the Well" and "The Lance" and you'll be rewarded with a **[Golden Egg]** for your help.

Now go speak with the boy a house down and you'll trigger the Side Quest *A Curious Child*.

Spawn a *Zol* in front of him, then an *Ignizol*, then a *Hydrozol*, and finally spawn another *Hydrozol* and place a *water block* on it to make it bigger. He'll give you a [Might Crystal] for finishing this Side Quest!

**066/150 Collected!** ☐

Warp to the Waypoint in *Zora Cove*, go into the village, speak with the Zora here, and then go outside and find them an **empty treasure chest** for the *Precious Treasure* Side Quest.

Grab one from the Sea Urchins and drop it in front of him on land for **3 x [Monster Stones]**.

Now quickly swim West to trigger another Side Quest: *Big Shot*. Cast your Chompfin Echo and clear out all the monsters before speaking with him on the boat.

After he gives you **10 x [Riverhorses]** as a reward, speak with the old man standing on top of the boat by the water's edge.

Make your way South to the wrecked ship, climb on board with a water column, and pull off the wooden plank with Bind.

## Wrecked Ship

This is a mini-dungeon (with a mini-boss at the end), so let's do it.

Pull the crates away from the wall in the top-right corner of the room to reveal some steps leading down.

Ignore the enemies in the next room, and keep walking left and down. In the next room, go left and open up the chest in the left-hand corner for **5 x [Rocktatoes]**.

Put on your *Zora Scale* and then dive down into the water. There's a chest down here with **50 Rupees** in it.

Swim left, up, then right, then up, exit the water, the chest has **5 x [Electro Apples]**.

Build a water column to get up onto the broken wall, jump into the water, and lay some boxes down, grab the statue with Bind and then jump up and left to drop it on the switch.

Go through the door, ignore the enemies, head up the steps, then go left for the boss fight.

## 1st Phase

For this battle, we **strongly** recommend that you take a *Shock Resistance* smoothie/potion at the start of the fight to give you the edge.

Attack wise, we brought out the trusty *Ball-and-Chain Trooper* Echo, as we could walk around with it using **Bind**, allowing it to hit the mini jellyfishes, while along us to move around safely. But any, sturdy, long-range Echo will be useful.

When it goes down, switch to *Swordfighter* mode, and lay into it as fast as you can.

## 2nd Phase

For phase two, the mini jellyfish will take up more room in an already small arena. Keep using your echo to take out the mini jellyfish first, and once they're down, one more series of good *Swordfighter* hits should see this mini-boss go down for good.

Collect the Rupees and the **[Piece of Heart]** before warping out.

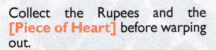

Speak with the man again to be rewarded with a **[Fairy Bottle]**!

After completing the *Zappy Shipwreck* Sub Quest, warp to the *River Zora Village* Waypoint.

Travel upwards to the Northeast looking for a cracked wall (just up and left from the Rift). Blow it to find a chest with **50 Rupees**.

Now make your way down to said Rift and step inside it.

# STILLED EASTERN ZORA RIVER

There's only three Energy Orbs to find here so, let's get to it.

## Energy Orb 1

Head North, into the water, then immediately go West. The far-left island holds the Energy Orb on top of a tree.

## Energy Orb 2

Now head East and then North to the cave with the ladder. After dropping off the ladder, go West (using a Flying Tile), and claim the Energy Orb in the water.

## Energy Orb 3

Immediately travel Eastward (through all the water) and look for the glowing fish in the water.

Use a Bombfish to kill it and claim the third and final Energy Orb here!

Tri will now level up a bit more and give you **2 x [Might Crystals]** as a reward.

068/150 Collected!

After exiting the Rift, warp to the *Gerudo Desert Entrance* Waypoint. Equip your Gerudo Sandals, and then walk North-west where you'll trigger another mini-boss battle…

This boss fight is **a lot** easier if you've purchased the **Gerudo Sandals** from the *Gerudo Town Shop* as you won't sink into the sand!

For the return battle, the method remains pretty much the same. Once it pops up out of the sand, latch onto its tail with **Bind** and then quickly get up close and hit it with as many sword swings as you possibly can before it flips back over again.

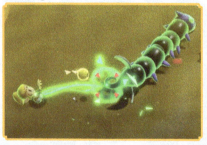

There's also no real "phases" as the boss simply pops up and goes back down into the sand, no matter how many times you hit it.

Depending on the strength of your sword, this battle can take anywhere from three to five rounds to finish.

Warp to *Gerudo Town* and speak with the Gerudo standing by the unlit torch to start the *Beetle Ballyhoo* Side Quest.

Head outside, go right, and speak with *Dohna* to trigger *Dohna's Challenge*.

Climb on top of the treasury and dig a hole in the sand pit in the roof to get inside.

The chest just up ahead contains **10 x [Chilly Cactus]**, if you go for it, be wary of needing to run away from the guards when they spot you!

You can use your Tile to travel on the top of the vase shelves and as long as the Gerudo guarding the chest at the top isn't looking, open it for the **[Silk Pajamas]**!

After completing this Side Quest, you can switch to your new Silk Pajamas as wearing them while sleeping in your own bed will rapidly recover any lost health!

Now walk to the opening just to the left of the main Gerudo Palace and speak with the left-hand guard here to start the *Wild Sandstorms* Side Quest.

Immediately warp back to the *Gerudo Desert Entrance* Waypoint and go North-west again to see the Lanmola re-appear!

## Lanmola (Final Battle)

Keep it simple and use your Swordfighter sword to hack away at it after pulling it out of the sand. This time though, you'll be rewarded with a [Piece of Heart] for defeating it!

16/40 Collected? ◻

Warp to the *Oasis*, and head inside the tent to do the **Ultimate Seeds** test (turn to page 243 for the full strategy there). However, make sure to have your *Frog Ring* equipped as it'll make jumping up into the corners **much** quicker!

Clearing the hardest level will earn you the **[Dancing Outfit]**, 12 x **[Tough Mangoes]** and clear all **70** for a [Piece of Heart].

17/40 Collected? ◻

Immediately head East from the tent and enter the cave entrance in the cliff face.

Destroy the mounds in here to complete the *Beetle Ballyhoo* Side Quest and warp back to the *Gerudo Town* to let her know. Earning you the **[Heart Barrette]**. Awesome!

Go back to the guard in the palace to let them know the *Lanmola* is finally gone. You'll be rewarded with the **[Gold Sash]** accessory.

Now warp to the Waypoint which is on the North-western edge of the unexplored part of the map.

Immediately travel South, climb up, then go left and enter the Rift here.

# STILLED NORTHERN GERUDO DESERT

There's **four** Energy Orbs to find here so, let's get to it.

## Energy Orb 1

Inside the cave, drop a Boulder and use your sword on the ReDead as the tiles hit the boulder. Collect the Energy Orb.

## Energy Orb 2

Exit the cave, go right, fly across the gap, then go up, then travel right to the lone island. Use a Wind-cannon on the sand here to reveal the next Energy Orb.

## Energy Orb 3

Go left, climb up the wall, fly left and the Energy Orb is waiting there for you.

## Energy Orb 4

The final Energy Orb is to the far left. Fly across and then take out both Moblins to make the final Energy Orb appear!

If you've been following our guide closely, then Tri will now be Level 6! This grants Tri one extra triangle for summoning Echoes with. Tri also gives you **2 x** [Might Crystals] as a thank you.

070/150 Collected!

Once you leave the Rift, warp to the Southern Waypoint of *Hyrule Field*.

Head South, and quickly clear out the Moblin camp here for a chest containing 10 x [Fresh Milk].

Now proceed North, into the mini-woods, and grab the [Piece of Heart] that's just sitting there on the tree stump.

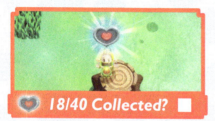

18/40 Collected?

From here, go into the top-left corner of the woods and dig a hole in the sand here to reveal a hidden [Might Crystal]!

071/150 Collected!

From here, proceed Westward towards *Hyrule Ranch*. Activate the **Waypoint** here and then claim the [Stamp Stand] nearby.

11/25 Located!

Speak with the old man in the ranch and you'll start the *Runaway Horse* Side Quest.

Run North-west (past all the Tektites and rocky mounds), but keep an eye out on the right for a suspicious circle of rocks. Lift the middle one for a hidden [Might Crystal].

072/150 Collected!

From here, go West and clear out the Moblin camp for a chest containing 10 x [Electro Apples]. From the Moblin camp, proceed South to the little pool of water with Octoroks. Use a Tile to reach the central pillar with the [Piece of Heart] on it.

19/40 Collected?

Fly South from the pillar and spin into the lone bush near the cliff face for a [Might Crystal].

073/150 Collected!

From the Crystal, head East and go into the rocky cave entrance. Clear out the Moblins and open the chest for 3 x [Might Crystals].

076/150 Collected!

Leave the cave, go South-east and you'll see that the runaway horse is on a small island surrounded by water. Use Bind to pull it to land, and ride it South-east to a little mound of grass.

Cut the lone bush to reveal a hidden [Might Crystal].

077/150 Collected!

Now ride North-east and deliver the horse back to the Ranch to complete the Side Quest and gain free access to ride any of the regular horses!

Immediately head North-east from the Ranch to see a cut-scene of a face that should be instantly recognizable to all long-term Zelda fans!

This starts the Side Quest *Automation Engineer Dampé*. Get rid of the Crow and then head Eastward. Look for the rock mound surrounded by Ignizols, and clear the bush for a hidden [Might Crystal].

**078/150 Collected!** ☐

From here, go North-west to the next **Waypoint** and activate it. Just up and to the right of the Waypoint are four boulders surrounded by grass. Lift the central boulder for a hidden [Might Crystal].

**079/150 Collected!** ☐

From here, go North-east to see some steps leading down in the middle of some ruins.

Head down and collect the [Might Crystal] just laying on the ground! Silly place to leave it!

**080/150 Collected!** ☐

Head back outside, go North, and be sure to grab the [Piece of Heart] from the top of the pillar here.

**20/40 Collected?** ☐

Just off to the left of here is a half-buried chest containing **5 x [Rocktatoes]** if you want them.

Continue in a North/North-easterly direction until you reach the **Waypoint** just outside the *Eternal Forest*.

For now, go South (back towards *Hyrule Castle*), and go speak with *Impa* who's in the main chamber. This triggers the *Impa's Gift* Side Quest.

From here, Warp to *Hyrule Ranch*, and speak with the girl here to progress Impa's Side Quest. Now warp to the Northern-most Waypoint (North-west of *Hyrule Castle*), and then head South towards the Rift.

Tri will create an entrance here for you to go in.

# STILLED CARROT PATCH

There's **four** Energy Orbs to find here so, let's get to it.

## Energy Orb 1

Head North, then move the top-right corner box away to reveal some steps. Climb down, use Bind and the Platboom to lift the large Boulder up and onto the switch. Break the crates for the Orb.

## Energy Orb 2

Head back outside, go North, climb up the wall with a Crawtula, and go left for the next Orb.

## Energy Orb 3

Drop down the South-western pillars onto the grass patch.

Use Bind to move the Boulders to reveal the next Orb at the top.

## Energy Orb 4

Head South-east from here and lift up the bottom-left crate to reveal some steps down.

Clear out both Moblins to make the fourth, and final, Energy Orb appear!

As per usual, Tri gains some more power and you'll be given **2 x [Might Crystals]** as thanks.

**082/150 Collected!**

If you've been following our guide closely, then you'll have collected more than half of the 150 Might Crystals in the game! Nice work! Let's keep going!

Once you exit the Rift, pull a carrot out with Bind and then be sure to learn the **Carrot Echo** while you're here!

▽ **075/127 Learned!** ☐

Warp back to *Hyrule Ranch*, go in, drop a carrot, and your white horse will show up. If you speak to the girl, you can now take part in the *Flag Races* mini-game!

For a full breakdown of how to win at all three courses, see page 243 near the back of our guide.

If you beat the *Short Course* in under 17 seconds, you'll get **3 x** **[Might Crystals]**.

♦ **085/150 Collected!** ☐

Successfully completing the *Middle Course* will earn you the **[Prismatic Music Box]** and beating it in under 20 seconds earns you a **[Piece of Heart]**!

♥ **21/40 Collected?** ☐

If you're feeling confident, then using the shortcuts on the *Long Course* we mention on page 244, will earn you **[50 Rupees]** and for beating it in under 40 seconds, you'll earn **[The Charging Horn]** accessory!

Activate the new **Waypoint** located just North-west of the Ranch, then open the chest surrounded by stones a bit further West for a **[Monster Stone]**.

It's time to use those ingredients and make some smoothies! Fly North-west some more until you reach the Business Shrub by the trees.

We recommend you make a couple of smoothies by mixing some *Peppers* and *Milk* (*Warm Mixed Special*) and something like *Grapes* and a *Monster Fang* (an *Unfortunate Smoothie*).

Head North-east and activate the **[Stamp Stand]** just outside the legendary *Kakariko Village*.

12/25 Located!

Head inside the village store and buy the **[Climbing Band]** for 500 Rupees.

Climbing Band    500

*Wall-Climb Speed Up*

*A leather band that protects your wrist. Wear it to climb ladders and rock walls faster.*

Save yourself time and pick up the *Cucco* by your feet, head left with it, activate the **Waypoint**, pick the Cucco back up and drop it by the woman with the wooden pen.

Speak with her to start the *Cuccos on the Loose* Side Quest. Throw the Cucco with you into the pen, then look South-west for the next Cucco in the yellow flower patch, throw that in next.

If you want **3 x [Refreshing Grapes]** you can lift the lid of the well off and jump down for a chest.

Feel free to speak to the old man near the well to trigger the *Questioning the Local Cats* Side Quest.

Lift up the Cucco by the old man and throw it in the pen. That's 3/5 down, two to go!

Speak with the woman outside the village shop, then head up to the Windmill in the North-east part of the village. Use a *Grilled Fish Echo* to lure the cat off the patch of dirt.

Use your *Holmill* to dig the patch and claim the bag of Rupees. In return you'll get given the **[Cat Clothes]**.

Put the Cat Clothes on, then get on top of the Windmill to find a cheeky **Cucco on the roof**! Take it back to the pen, then head up to the graveyard and dig a hole left of the graves for a **[Might Crystal]**.

086/150 Collected!

Speak with the cat on top of the Windmill to the left, then take the final Cucco at the Graveyard to the pen to complete the *Cuccos on the Loose* Side Quest, earning you a **[Fairy Bottle]** as a reward!

Exit *Kakariko Village* via the right-hand path and look for a cat perched up on a tree. Talk to it then look for a small patch of dirt by the trees (just above the nearby cave entrance).

Dig in to drop down into the cave beside a **[Piece of Heart]**.

22/40 Collected?

While you're here, fly right, and carefully learn the ***Spiked-roller Echo*** (this one is good for clearing out those Moblin camps). Continue right and use the Spiked Roller to clear out the boxes, and open the chest for a **[Golden Egg]**.

076/127 Learned!

Exit the cave, then jump up the mounds to the North to find the *Acorn Gathering* mini-game man!

Full tips can be found on page 240, however, make sure your *Frog Ring* is still in your accessory slot for quickly reaching the Acorns in the trees.

Beating it under 25 seconds will earn you a **[Piece of Heart]**.

23/40 Collected?

Go back to *Kakariko Village* and speak with the Old Man to complete his Side Quest and you'll get **10 x [Refreshing Grapes]**.

Head to the far left of the village and enter the *Slumber Dojo*.

This is another major mini-game (one with a *lot* of levels to go through), so please **check out page 244** for a guide on how to beat *every single Dojo training level*!

If you've been following our guide closely, then there'll be **six** challenges unlocked for you to try. The others will unlock later (don't worry, we'll let you know when to come back for the rest).

24/40 Collected? ☐

Blank-Slate Battle
Caromadillos' Revenge
Flow of Battle
Blank-Slate Battle: Wind
Titans' Gathering
Moblins' Revenge

Blank-Slate Ba

Start with no echoes and n
allowed. Defeat your enem
only what's available in the

Goal Time
Best Time

If you do all six challenges now, you'll earn the following rewards:

- *5 x Electro Apples*
- *5 x Jars of Floral Nectar (speed bonus)*
- *5 x Monster Fangs*
- *3 x Refreshing Grapes (Speed Bonus)*
- *[Piece of Heart]*
- *5 x Bubble Kelp*
- *5 x Riverhorses (speed bonus)*
- *5 x Chilly Cactus*
- *5 x Warm Peppers (speed bonus)*
- **[First Mastery Accessory]**
- *5 x Fresh Milk*
- *7 x Radiant Butter*
- *3 x Monster Stones*
- **[Heirloom Katana]**!

Leave the Dojo and head North to tackle the first of the three key areas remaining: *Eldin Volcano!*

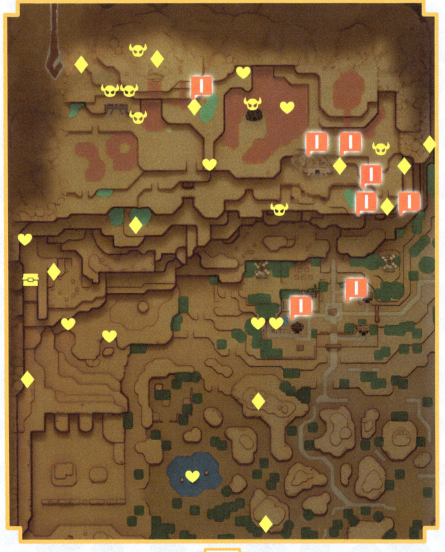

# ELDIN VOLCANO RIFT

## It's time to rock and roll!

Once Tri has finished looking around, head left and then go in the cave. Kill/dodge all of the Beetles and then open the chest for **5 x [Rocktatoes]**.

Use Bind to pull the fiery slug off of the wall and kill it with Arrows and learn the *Torch Slug Echo*.

▽ 078/127 *Learned!* ☐

Go up, activate the **Waypoint** here, drop down the South-west ledge to see a cracked wall. Use a Bombfish on it to open it.

▽ 077/127 *Learned!* ☐

Keep going left and clear out the camp of *Lizalfos* and open the chest for **3 x [Might Crystals]**.

💎 089/150 *Collected!* ☐

Open the chest for a **[Fairy Flower]** accessory! Immediately run South and lift up the lone rock for a **[Might Crystal]**.

💎 090/150 *Collected!* ☐

Go up a bit and be sure to claim your next **[Stamp Stand]** too.

**13/25 Located!**

Look for a small round patch of dirt just North-east of the Stamp Stand (above the cave entrance), dig a hole in here to drop down beside a **[Piece of Heart]**!

**25/40 Collected?**

Walk Eastward and look for a large Boulder between the grass and the sand. Use a Platboom to Bind and lift the Boulder up, revealing another **[Piece of Heart]**. Sneaky!

**26/40 Collected?**

Now make a run for the top North-west corner of the volcano and there's a tall, but small, platform there with a **[Piece of Heart]** perched on it. Use a Crawltula to reach it easily.

**27/40 Collected?**

From here, head Eastward, and make a beeline for the large nearby Rift entrance. Tri will open it up for you.

# STILLED WESTERN ELDIN VOLCANO

There's a total of **five** Energy Orbs to find here. So, let's get to it.

## Energy Orb 1

Immediately go right and kill the flying enemy with Arrows, then learn the *Ghirro Echo*.

079/127 Learned!

Use the Ghirro and the wind to fly around the still area quickly. The Orb is on the route around.

## Energy Orb 2

Head left then use some Arrows to quickly kill the *Fire Wizzrobe*.

080/127 Learned!

The Orb is in the left-hand corner near the lava.

## Energy Orb 3

Head North-east and go down the steps. Drop down to the left and kill the enemy here for the Orb.

## Energy Orb 4

Stay in the cave, go to the bottom, kill the enemies here and collect the fourth Orb.

## Energy Orb 5

From the fourth Orb, use the warm air to lift you up the right-hand side to the final Orb.

Tri powers up and you'll earn another **2 x [Might Crystals]**.

092/150 Collected!

*Top Tip! Standing in any of the green hot springs will slowly replenish your health if you're hurt.*

Once you exit the Rift, drop down the cliff to your right and enter the cave entrance here.

Use your new Ghirro Echo to blow out all of the flames here. Keep going right, and climb up the wall to the chest for another **[Monster Stone]**.

Go up the cliff and near the central Rift is a **[Stamp Stand]**.

Head left from here for a new **Waypoint**. Go up and speak with the *Goron* to progress the Main Quest-line. Head inside to enter the Rift here.

# STILLED GORON CITY

There's a total of **four** energy orbs to find here. So, let's get to it.

## Energy Orb 1

Go up and kill the *Zirro* that's flying around, chucking bombs everywhere!

▼ **081/127 Learned!** ☐

Climb down ladder in the big Goron pot and use bombs to reach the Orb at the bottom.

## Energy Orb 2

Head North-west after exiting the Goron pot and the Orb is on a platform.

## Energy Orb 3

The third Orb isn't far away. It's located just to the West, high up.

## Energy Orb 4

The final Orb can be found by traveling South and dropping down the cliffs to the platform it's on.

Tri will powers-up and you'll receive **2 x** [Might Crystals] for your help.

💎 **094/150 Collected!** ☐

## The Rift on Eldin Volcano

Once the cut-scene ends, head outside and you'll be tasked with finding two Gorons.

Once you regain control of Zelda, immediately go right and look for a large drop down to a chest on the cliff edge.

Drop down to the chest and open it for **2 x [Might Crystals]**.

096I50 Collected!

Now use a flying Echo to float down to the **[Stamp Stand]** on the cliff edge to the right.

15/25 Located!

If you've be following our guide closely, then this stamp will earn you a **[Fairy Bottle]**! Sweet!

You need to drop down to the small platform on the right. Pick up the rock for a **[Might Crystal]**.

097 /150 Collected!

Glide from here down and to the left. There's a cracked wall in the cliff face for you to blow up, inside are **6 x [Monster Fangs]**.

Warp back to the top of the volcano, head North-east towards the hot lava ground, and kill a *Tweelus* with a strong Echo.

082/127 Learned!

Go up and left from here and kill the *Fire Octo* for its Echo.

**083/127 Learned!**

There's a chest here as well with a **[Golden Egg]** inside!

Go West from here and by the lava lake, there's a new rock platform, the **Lava Rock Echo**.

**084/127 Learned!**

In the center of the lava lake there's a **[Piece of Heart]**. Use a Flying Tile to easily reach it.

**28/40 Collected?**

Fly to the right, then run around the outskirts of the lava field to the left to find a new **Waypoint**.

Head inside the Goron building.

## Lizalfos Burrow

Enter the burrow and ready your strongest Echo to use against the Lizalfos.

Grab the **5 x [Rocktatoes]** from the chest, then in the next room dispatch the two **Lizalfos Lv. 2**.

**085/127 Learned!**

Use your Arrows in the next room as there's some **Fire Keese** in here flying around, causing havoc.

**086/127 Learned!**

Use Bind on the Dark Echoes in the large room to hold them as your main Echo deals with them.

## Rock-Roast Quarry

Alright, head West when exiting and use a Platboom to reach the upper level. Go down and grab the **[Piece of Heart]** resting here.

❤ **29/40 Collected?** ☐

Continue heading West from here, as there's a **[Stamp Stand]** sitting in between the lava and the Rift.

👤 **16/25 Located!** ☐

Head North and activate the **Waypoint** by *Rock-Roast Quarry*.

Head inside and use your Swordfighter form to quickly clear the room of enemies.

Learn the *Rock Roast Echo*, then open the nearby chest for **5 x [Rocktatoes]**.

▽ **087/127 Learned!** ☐

Now use Bind to drop one of the *real* Rock-Roasts by the Gorons at the entrance. Head back and grab one more for the group. Now warp back to the *Goron City*

Waypoint and then head upstairs and pull the bolt off.

## Hidden Shortcut

Alright, use your flying Echoes to use the warm jets of air to fly through each of the lava-filled rooms. The Platboom is also useful when you see jets of lava shooting up and you need a platform.

Make sure to use Bind and the Platbooms in tandem to cross the lava pits.

In the far-left of the lava jet room there's a chest with **50 Rupees**. However, ride a lava rock up the lava that shoots high into the air to reach the ladder that's out of sight.

Head on up and then activate the **Waypoint** beside the big Rift entrance.

# STILLED ELDIN VOLCANO

This Rift is the entrance to the dungeon for this region. So, thankfully, it's not too long to navigate.

If you use for Flying Tiles to travel North-east then there's a chest here with **5 x [Rocktatoes]** in them.

If you want some Rupees, then continue in a North and North-westerly direction where a **Waypoint** and a chest (located South-west from the Waypoint, lower down) holds **50 Rupees**.

Otherwise, keep pushing Northwards and use the warm air to fly past most of the annoying lava traps!

Eldin Temple

3F

2F

1F

Map

Set Pin

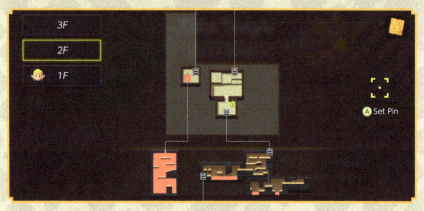

3F

2F

1F

Set Pin

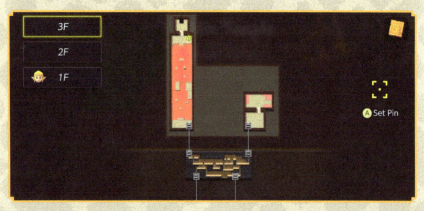

3F

2F

1F

Set Pin

Activate the **Waypoint**, go up, then right, then use a Platboom to reach the upper door on the right.

Now use a flying Echo to gain enough height to reach the chest with the **[Small Key]** inside.

Go back to the room with the Fire Keese, then head through the Northern door.

Dispatch the Dark Echoes, blow up the blocks in the top-right corner, and pull out the chest which contains **8 x [Twisted Pumpkins]**.

Go through the locked door and **very quickly** use a Lava Rock to reach the sunken chest when the lava level drops. You have to pull it out super fast if you want the **[Golden Egg]** that's inside!

Use a Lava Rock on the switch to the left of the room, then exit via the top right-hand corner.

In the side-on part, use a Tile to cross the upper level, then a

couple of Lava Rocks to ride the lava jets up. Push a Boulder against the air, and climb down the ladder on the right.

In the next room, the lava rises and falls, so you have to - quickly - hit the switch on the left (use an arrow), and then ride some Boulders when the lava rises to stay on the upper level.

The room on the right has a **[Small Key]** inside the chest. Go left, back up the ladder, then keep going upwards when in the side-on view.

To make it past the hot fire jets while climbing, bind a statue to you and then climb up. The statue will stop the fire from hitting you.

Repeat this tactic on the left-hand side, climb the ladder, then open the chest for the **[Dungeon Map]**. Climb the ladder, activate the **Waypoint**, and open up the door.

## 1st Phase

Dark Link returns and this time he's packing bombs!

We **strongly** recommend that you are wearing the *Frog Ring* in this fight as you'll want to be able to jump up the different levels as quickly as possible. You *can* use *Swordfighter* mode, but it's more hassle than just using the ring.

Follow the fake Link around the arena and once he stops, hit him as quickly as you can with the sword.

A few more hits like this (which will require you following him around the room, dodging bombs), will send him to phase two.

## 2nd Phase

This time, Link busts out the classic *Bombchus*! You **can't** turn these into Echoes we're afraid, but they *can* cause you serious damage if they explode near you!

They go in a straight line, so try to anticipate their paths while you make your way back to Dark Link. Get in as many hits with your sword as you can while dodging all the bombs.

It shouldn't take too many hits to see this Dark Link going down, giving you access to the **[Bombs]**!

Once you've got the bombs, go up the ladder, climb up, then look for the cracked blocks up on the right-hand side.

Blow them up, jump across, go right, then head up the ladder.

In the next room, clear the enemies, then bomb the top-left corner for a chest containing a handy **100 Rupees**! Bomb the right-hand corner to reveal the exit.

Use your strongest flying Echo in the next room as you need to defeat a Fire Wizzrobe to reveal a chest with the **[Small Key]** in it.

Head back down the ladder, then go left, hack away at the Dark Web,

Blow up all of the blocks below it as it's hiding a chest with another **[Small Key]** inside.

Go open the locked door that's just below you on the left, go down, and down again, and in the lava room, stick to the left hand side and climb down to the Big Chest with the **[Big Key]** inside.

You now have to be super quick as the lava rises fast! Climb back up to the ladder at the top, use a Tile to fly left when the ladder breaks, and exit the room before the lava gets you!

Go up the ladders, blow the cracked blocks on the left, climb this ladder up, open the next locked door, and in this long lava room, use the *Ghirro Echo* to catch the wind that pushes you up, allowing you to reach the other side without touching the lava.

Activate the **Waypoint** and get ready for a fiery boss fight!

## 1st Phase

The trick in this fight is to use **Bind** to pull off the **green necklace** which give the boss its powers.

It'll first appear in the top-left lava hole, where you need to dodge the green energy ball, before hitting it with your sword in *Swordfighter* mode.

## 2nd Phase

For phase two, it'll fly around then re-appear in the top-right lava hole, so get up close and hit it lots.

Be careful when it re-appears in the bottom-right corner lava hole as the energy ball is now faster, and the boss will take a swing at you. Once you break the necklace this time, use **ranged** attacks such as **Arrows** or **Bombs** to hit it.

## 3rd Phase

For phase three, be super careful of its lava stream attack! Try and bait it to use it on an upper level, before dropping down to pull on the necklace and use ranged attacks again to damage it.

Take your time and follow it around the arena, using long range shots when it's too far away to hit with your sword.

Also, watch out for the series of fireballs it'll fire at you in quick succession, this is your cue that you're nearing the end of the fight!

Keep it up and victory will soon be yours.

Tri's energy will see a massive jump (hopefully up to Level 7 where even more Echoes cost less to spawn in) and you'll earn another **5 x [Might Crystals]** too!

102/150 Collected!

You earn **10 x [Rock Salt]** for completing it. If you do the next flying course straight after, you can start the *Glide Path Trailblazer* Side Quest.

The Ghirro is your friend here as it can move around the air streams as well as dodge the falling rocks!

Reach the end flag and you'll receive **2 x [Might Crystals]**.

104/150 Collected!

## Pick-up Collection Time!

Before we tackle the next dungeon, let's spend some time grabbing as many new items and Echoes as we can along the way.

If you head to the far right, there's a boy Goron standing by the cliff edge. Chat to him to start the *Glide Path* Side Quest.

You should be *well* used to using both the *Ghirro* Echo and the hot air, so this should be easy.

Jump off, and glide left. The Ghirro should push you far enough to get you to the flag safely.

Now speak with the Goron nearby to start the *Ready? Set? Goron!* Side Quest.

Finish this super fast by using a Platboom platform at the start to go up, then use a Flying Tile to reach the flag for **50 Rupees**.

Head inside, then go in the top-right room and *Basa* will ask you for some Blastpowder Soil, starting the *Firework Artist* Side Quest.

Immediately warp to the *Rock-Roast* Waypoint, run left, and pick up the twinkling yellow flowers for the **[Blastpowder Soil]**.

*You got some blastpowder soil!*

From here, go straight up (using a Platboom), clear the enemy, and collect the **[Might Crystal]** from the chest here.

105/150 Collected!

From here, go Eastward, to the top level, where you'll soon encounter your next **[Stamp Stand]**.

17/25 Located!

From here, drop down and speak with *Ondes* by the lava-fall. This starts *The Flames of Fortune* Side Quest.

The quickest route is to take it with Bind to the narrow cliff

where the Piece of Heart was, then use a Flying Tile to quickly travel East.

You should land right near the *Goron City Entrance* where you need to give *Limme* the coal.

You'll get **2 x [Might Crystals]** for your trouble.

107/150 Collected!

Head inside the city, and go back upstairs, hand the Blastpowder over to complete the Side Quest and earn **50 Rupees**. Don't forget to learn the *Firework Echo* too!

088/127 Learned!

Briefly leave the city, then go back in and speak with *Gol* to start the *A Mountainous Mystery* Side Quest.

Warp to the *Lizalfos Burrow* Waypoint, get up to the ledge to your left, then head up and into the cave in the rock face.

Once you enter the lava room, you can quickly skip most of the slow platforming by using a Flying Tile to zip between the climbing wall and the Lava Rocks below you.

Use a Ghirro in the next room to fly over all of the lava and flames on the ground below.

Climb up and down the ladders until you reach the far right. Just start dropping a series of Boulders to use them as platforms, riding the last one up to the top.

Once you reach the top, it's time for a mini-boss battle. You ready?

Make your way to the back of the room and head down the ladder.

Be careful and time your movements in the next room for when the lava goes down. The chest by the climbing wall has **50 Rupees** inside.

### 1st Phase

The first phase is very similar to the regular version of this boss you beat early on in the game. However, you have to use an **Extended Bind** to safely grab the orb, while dodging its fiery fists!

Use your sword to hack away at the orb once the boss crumbles into a heap.

### 2nd Phase

Like before, use an extended bind to pull the sphere away from the boss, whilst dodging its spinning arms of doom.

Make sure to get in close and hack away at the sphere with your sword to send it on to phase three.

### 3rd Phase

This time, equip your *Wind-cannon* Echo and get ready to drop it once the boss slams the ground. This blows out the flames, making it safer to pull the sphere out from the boss' head.

As before, hack away at the sphere with your sword and the boss will regenerate one final time, but the sphere will move to its back.

Simply repeat the previous step of using the *Wind-cannon* Echo to blow out the flames, then get behind it to pull the sphere out.

One more good series of hits with your sword should see this fight come to an end. Make sure to collect the [Piece of Heart] it drops!

**♥ 30/40 Collected?** ☐

Once you go back out, you'll also be given the **[Goron's Bracelet]** as a reward, nice one! We're done with the Volcano (for now), so warp to the Waypoint by the *Eternal Forest.*

## Echoes, Items, and Rifts

Head South to the smoothie Scrub and, if you have more than 10 Golden Eggs on you, sell him seven for 750 Rupees.

Now go North-east slightly and you should see a rather large Rift with an entrance. Let's rescue more of Hyrule shall we?

## STILLED NORTHERN SANCTUARY

There's a total of **three** energy orbs to find here. So, let's get to it.

## Energy Orb 1

Immediately head inside the Sanctuary and clear it of enemies to make the Energy Orb appear.

## Energy Orb 2

Exit the Sanctuary and go right. Look for the side-way gravestones and pull the top central one to the left to reveal the Energy Orb.

Before claiming the last Orb, it's worth dispatching the **Ghini** ghosts on the far right-side of the world. Use your Arrows and then learn their Echo while you're here.

▼ *089/127 Learned!*

## Energy Orb 3

The final Energy Orb is in the middle gravestone by the ghosts. Just pull it back to reveal it.

As per usual, Tri gains more energy and you get another **2 x [Might Crystals]** in return!

*109/150 Collected!*

Upon exiting the Rift, go speak with the Acorn Gathering man who's right outside!

Again, our mini-games section at the back of our guide on page 240 gives you a full breakdown. Just make sure to have your *Frog Ring* and narrow platform walking skills at the ready.

Do it quick enough and you'll earn yourself a **[Golden Egg]**.

Now go right and into the graveyard. Look for the large headstone surrounded by a fence and light the torches to reveal a staircase down.

Kill or dodge the ghosts here, and quickly learn the *Stuffed Toy Echo* as it sits on the box.

▼ *090/127 Learned!* ☐

In the next room, use a Ghini Echo while standing up against the back wall and send it into the switch.

Switch to Swordfighter mode and use a charged Arrow shot on the large, green *Ghini Lv. 2* that's here.

▼ *091/127 Learned!* ☐

Head right and grab the **[Golden Egg]** from the chest before leaving.

Go South and activate the **Waypoint** here. Head far East to the Moblin camp in *Eastern Hyrule Field*. Clear it out for a **[Monster Stone]** and a *Sword Moblin Lv. 2*.

▼ *092/127 Learned!* ☐

Continue going North in *Eastern Hyrule Field* until you reach Dampé's house.

# DAMPÉ AUTOMATION

 ## The Original Windup Merchant

Dampé has upgraded his dungeon building antics from his time in Link's Awakening, to turning his skills into building mechanical versions of the different Echos found in the game.

Let's take a closer look at how to trigger his major side-quest, along with what's required to unlock every Automation in the game.

### Side-Quest Unlock

You **must** first finish the *Still Missing* main quest. Once that's completed, you can look for Dampé standing near a tree just North of *Hyrule Ranch*.

Defeat the **Crow** for him, talk to him, then head to his house located North of *Eastern Hyrule Field*. Inside he'll thank you with **5 x [Twisted Pumpkins]**.

Let's look at how to help him build the rest of these Automations.

*Dampé*
Stop being a pest and gimme my key!

## Quest: Find Inspiration for Dampé

To complete this quest, you need to summon the following two Echoes on the pedestal in front of him:

1. A *Tektite (Seesyde Village)*
2. A *Mothula (Gerudo Sanctum)*

He'll now build you your very own mechanical version of the *Techtite* Echo.

## Quest: Explosions Galore

Two more Echoes are required. However, it's going to take a bit more effort to get the second one…

Step:

1. Present an *Octorok Echo*
2. Speak to *Basa* in **Goron City** up in **Eldin Volcano** and complete the *Fireworks Artist* side-quest.
3. Clone the *Fireworks* Echo here and then show Dampé it.

This unlocks the *Tocktorock!*

## Quest: Performance Artist

One Echo and an item are required for this. You don't *need* The **White Horse** to win the prize needed, but it'll certainly make it a *whole* lot easier!

Step:

1. Present a *Zol Echo*
2. You need to beat the middle *Flag Race Mini-game* course (ideally by using the **White Horse** from the side-quest *Impa's Gift*).
3. Give the **[Pristine Music Box]** from beating the middle course to Dampé to unlock the *Gizmol.*

## Quest: Endless Stomach

One Echo and a different item is required for the *High-Teku Baba Automaton*.

Step:

1. Present a *Deku Baba Echo*

2. You need to clear the *Stilled Northern Sanctuary Rift* and then speak with the guy by the church and ask him about a Clamp.

3. Head to the *Acorn mini-game* located in the far West of *Hyrule Field* and beat it in under **40 seconds** to earn the **[Clamp]**.

4. Hand it to Dampé and he'll build this Automation for you.

## Quest: Chop 'em In Two

This one is tougher as it requires you to use and Echo and also finish the - rather tough - *Slumber Dojo Training mini-game!*

Step:

1. Present a *Sword Moblin Echo*

2. Beat **every** Dojo training mission to earn the **[Heirloom Katana]**.

3. Present these to Dampé and he'll build you the *Robolin Automation*.

## Quest: Get Rich Quick

This requires one Echo and an item to make the *Goldfinch Automation*.

Step:

1. Present a Crow *Echo*

2. Collect **50 or more Vibrant Seeds** in the *Mango Rush mini-game* in the Oasis. (*Gerudo Desert*) for the **[Golden Fan]**.

3. Show both of these to Dampé to unlock this Automation.

Once you leave his home, go down a little and go up on the ledge by the Waypoint outside his home. There's a patch of sand you can dig up for a [Might Crystal].

110/150 Collected!

Head up from here and go into the cave entrance. Use an Echo (like a Platboom) on the Switch to open up access to the chest which has 3 x [Might Crystals] inside it.

113/150 Collected!

Leave the cave, go up the ledge on the left and lift up the lone rock for *another* [Might Crystal]!

114/150 Collected!

Go left from here, drop into the edge of the water and swim North-west until you reach the [Stamp Stand] on the island.

18/25 Located!

From here, go directly South to the small island and go down into the cave here.

Place a Platboom at the bottom of the water and ride it up to the chest for **3 x [Floral Nectar]**.

Go left, grab the yellow *Ribbitune* and kill it for its Echo.

093/127 Learned!

## Great Fairy Upgrades

Warp to the Great Fairy in *Lake Hylia* and you should have enough Rupees for a full upgrade. If not, sell a few more Golden Eggs and come back. Be sure to fill your Fairy Bottles while here too.

Leave the Fairy's home, then immediately re-enter to make a chest appear (now that there's no more accessory slots to buy). Inside is a [Might Crystal].

This starts the Side Quest *The Great Fairy's Request.*

Warp to *Gerudo Town* and enter the shop here. Talk to the shopkeeper and then immediately warp to *Goron City* and speak with the Goron shopkeeper.

Warp/head to *Lizalfos Burrow* and clear out the last room of the Lizalfos to earn the **[Magma Stone]**. One item down.

Now warp to the *Zora Cove* Waypoint and speak with the Zora just off to the right to trigger the *Secret Chief Talks* Side Quest.

Swim down and into the *Sea Zora Village* and speak with the shopkeeper here on the left. Give

them that **Unfortunate Smoothie** that you made much earlier, and you'll get the **[Floral Seashell]** in return.

Warp to the *River Zora Village* Waypoint and head into the Chief's hut. Speak to the Zora's out here, then fly with a Tile to the East to find *Tellum*.

Now warp back to *Zora Cove* and immediately head East, up to the Island with the broken corner. Head inside the cave's entrance.

After the cut-scene you'll be rewarded with the **[Gold Brooch]** and will complete the *Secret Chief Talks* Side Quest.

Put on your Cat Clothes and then warp to *Seesyde Village* and chat with the cat by the Waypoint to start the *A Treat for my Person* Side Quest.

Funnily enough, that *other* smoothie we had you make much earlier is **exactly** the one you need now! What are the odds?…

Your reward for completing this is a [Might Crystal].

Now warp back to *Gerudo Town* and hand the items to the shopkeeper here.

Warp back to the *Great Fairy* with the Pendant in-hand and you'll be rewarded with the **[Might Bell]**!

## More Echoes and Items

Our quest for 100% completion continues! Warp to *Hyrule Castle* and speak with the young Zol fan again outside his house to start the *An Out-There Zol* Side Quest.

Show him the *Gizmol* to complete this Side Quest immediately, you'll earn a **[Piece of Heart]**.

Now go up and speak with the girl to be given a **[Four-Leafed Clover]** to start the Side Quest *From the Heart*. Immediately take it to the King in the castle and then warp to the bottom *Hyrule Field* Waypoint. Head West and go to the Rift here.

# STILLED SOUTHERN HYRULE FIELD

There's a total of **three** energy orbs to find here. So, let's get to it.

## Energy Orb 1

Immediately head left, climb up the wall, then drop the glowing Dark Echo off the edge, collect the Orb

## Energy Orb 2

Go to the right from here and clear the island of all the Dark Echoes. Collect the Energy Orb that appears.

## Energy Orb 3

The final Orb isn't far away. Continue right until you see the water and then jump in.

Clear out the fish in here for the final Energy Orb!

Tri's energy will increase and you'll be rewarded with **2 x [Might Crystals]** for your troubles.

118/150 Collected! ■

Upon exiting the Rift, you'll also be rewarded with the **[Customary Attire]** from the King!

Now's a great time to double-check that you're using all your accessory slots and try on your new dress!

Warp to *Luberry's House* and, if you've been following our guide closely, ask him to upgrade **everything** (as you should have more than enough Might Crystals for the every available upgrade)!

Now that you're all upgraded, it's time to tackle the next major dungeon.

There's two corners of the map left for us to explore, the cold mountainous North, or the wet, Jungles of the South-east.

Main Quest  Accessory  Heart Piece

Side Quest  Enemy Echo  Might Crystal

# Faron Wetlands Rift

## Welcome to the Jungle (for fun and games)

Only two more major dungeons left to conquer before we can take a stab at saving Hyrule. Let's go! Check the map for the nearby Rift and make your way over the trees to it and enter.

## Stilled Lower Southern Forest

There's a total of **four** energy orbs to find here. So, let's get to it.

## Energy Orb 1

Immediately head right, clear out all the Dark Echoes and grab the Orb from on top of the trees.

## Energy Orb 2

From here, travel to the far-left side and use a platform and clear the Moblins to claim the next Energy Orb.

## Energy Orb 3

From here, head North-east, climb up on top of the sideways land, go up, then fly across to the Orb on the island with trees.

## Energy Orb 4

Simply drop down and right, smash open the three wooden crates here for the fourth, and final, Energy Orb in this Rift!

As always, Tri's energy increases (by now, our Tri was **Level 8**) and you get **2 x** [Might Crystals].

120/150 Collected! ■

Once you exit the Rift, start heading due East to the pathway on the map that sits in between *Suthorn Forest* and *Faron Wetlands*.

There's a single bush surrounded by trees. Cut it for a hidden [Might Crystal].

▼ 121/150 Collected! ☐

The chest in the Moblin camp just North of here holds **10 x [Refreshing Grapes]**.

If you follow the dirt path from the Moblin camp North, there's another Moblin camp with a chest containing **7 x [Riverhorses]**.

## A Rift in the Faron Wetlands

From this chest, go South-east and drop down into the Jungle that is *Faron Wetlands*. Activate the **Waypoint** here.

Go through the pathway here, and have your favorite, strongest Echo at the ready.

Be sure to learn the Echo for the blue *Drippitune* frog that's on the tree stump.

▼ 094/127 Learned! ☐

Once you reach the two small Deku Scrubs, head South, and look out for the **[Stamp Stand]** that's sitting in the small pool of water.

👤 19/25 Located! ☐

Continue in a North-easterly direction until you see the small Scrub on its own on broken stone blocks. Speak with it to start *The Rain-Making Monster* Side Quest.

Immediately show it the *Drippitune Echo* you've just caught to complete it for a reward of **8 x [Electro Apples]**.

Open the nearby chest for **5 x [Radiant Butter]**. Continue right and enter the *Smoothie Shop*.

Ask him to combine **Radiant Butter + Monster Fang** for a **Radiant Potion**.

Head North-west from the Smoothie Shop and activate the **Waypoint** here.

Go North up to the locked door and you'll be told you need a **Membership Card** to get in!

Continue East until you see those bright blue mushrooms on the ground. Some of them are enemies in disguise! Kill one and learn the *Hoarder Echo*.

▼ 095/127 Learned! ☐

Watch out for the small red spiders by the Rift's edge. Kill one for the *Baby Gohma Echo*.

▼ 096/127 Learned! ☐

Go to the North-east corner (use a Platboom to get up), where you'll find a [Stamp Stand] waiting.

👤 20/25 Located! ☐

Just off to the left, use a Platboom and a Brazier on top to burn the web on the wall, and access the [Might Crystal].

💎 122/150 Collected! ☐

Drop down and use some Arrows on the *Buzz Blobs* below. Their electrical range is amplified when they get wet (rain, puddles, or underwater). Super handy to use!

▼ 097/127 Learned! ☐

Head directly South from here and look for the long grass. Grab the head of the nearest *Deku Baba Lv. 2* and pull it back to kill it.

▼ 098/127 Learned! ☐

Continue South through the grass, go East, and take out the *Goo Specter* here for their Echo.

▼ 099/127 Learned! □

Continue East, then head North. Enter into the building for a mini-dungeon.

## Echo... Echo... Echo...

There's even *more* new Echoes to learn in here (along with a nice item at the end). Let's get to it!

Go up the second-from-the-left path to the statue. Once it wakens up, come back a bit, then use Bind on it to turn it around. Attack the vulnerable back and claim the **Armos Echo**.

▼ 100/127 Learned! □

Go down the ladder, then use **two** bombs on the blue **Beamos** enemy.

▼ 101/127 Learned! □

The chest down here contains **5 x [Electro Apples]**. Head up the ladders and you'll encounter quite a tough enemy at the end.

Lock-on to it and keep spamming your strongest Echo to take it down ASAP. Now go learn the **Darknut Lv. 3 Echo**!

▼ 102/127 Learned! □

Open the chest at the end for the **[Spin Brace]** accessory. Go down the ladder, head left, hit the switch, go down, and exit the building.

Go directly South from here (over a few sets of trees) and you'll soon encounter a stronger *Mothula* type. Kill it and learn the **Mothula Lv. 2 Echo**.

▼ 103/127 Learned! □

Go West and look for where the small Rift is on the map. To the South-east of the Rift (on a ledge) is a **[Stamp Stand]**.

**21/25 Located!** □

From here, go North (over the trees) and look for the pink bird. Take one out so you can learn the *Beakon Echo*.

▼ **104/127 Learned!** □

Continue West from here and look for a large puddle of water. There's a couple of new enemies in here. First, there's the *Piranha* and also the *Giant Goponga Flower Echoes*!

▼ **105/127 Learned!** □

▼ **106/127 Learned!** □

Continue in a North-westerly direction until you encounter loads of webs on the cliffs.

Check the map for a circular patch of green grass on the West side and make your way there (through the long grass).

You'll see some red and green plants. Cut the middle one for a hidden [Might Crystal].

**123/150 Collected!** □

From here, go East (over the trees) and go down the ladder of the nearby cave entrance. Equip both of your *Zora Accessories* for this underwater cave!

Spin swim your way through, use Bind on the statues to turn them around, making them easy to kill, then use a Platboom at the top to reach the platform with the [Piece of Heart] on it.

**32/40 Collected?** □

Jump back into the water and swim right. Use Bind to - quickly - pull the Boulders up and out of your way (this is why you want to wear the *Zora Accessories*!).

Once you reach the next, large screen, bring your *Chompfin* out and use it against the, strong, **Lizalfos Lv. 3**!

107/127 Learned!

Learn this as it's **super** powerful against underwater foes and it'll prove *especially* useful against the very last boss…

Exit the cave and immediately head South. Jump over some trees and you'll find a **[Stamp Stand]** on a small ledge.

22/25 Located!

Head further South (towards the far South-western corner of *Faron Wetlands* and activate he **Waypoint** here.

Go left and enter the Rift here.

# STILLED HEART LAKE

There's a total of **five** energy orbs to find here. So, let's get to it.

## Energy Orb 1

Head North at the entrance, clear the enemies, then burn the web to gain access to the Energy Orb.

## Energy Orb 2

This Orb is to the East of the first. Climb along the wall, set the web on fire, then claim the Orb.

## Energy Orb 3

Climb straight up from here, and burn the next spider's web for the third Energy Orb.

## Energy Orb 4

From here, go West until you see a pool of green water. Swim down the middle, and use Bind on a Bombfish to reach the Orb.

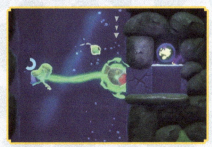

## Energy Orb 5

Thankfully, the final Energy Orb is located in the same area. Pull the Deku's head off, then swim up to the Orb to collect it.

Tri gains more power and you get an extra **2 x** [Might Crystals] for all your effort.

125/150 Collected!

## The Search Continues

With that membership card still alluding us, it's time to grab a few more key items as we aim to finish this adventure 100%.

Look East on the map for the large(ish) Rift. Just to the East of there is a cave, head there and go inside.

Use your Frog Ring and Braziers to get around the dark rooms. If you burn all the webs, then there's a chest with **50 Rupees** waiting for you.

The South end of this dark cave also has a [Piece of Heart] waiting on the right-hand side.

❤️ **33/40 Collected?** ⬜

Exit the cave via the right-hand exit, then go up to the ledge above you. Cut the middle plant for a [Might Crystal].

💎 **126/150 Collected!** ⬜

Be careful when going down here, as there's an **Electric Wizzrobe** flying around. Hold it with bind while you use your strongest aerial Echo on it.

▼ **108/127 Learned!** ⬜

Keep going East and activate the **Waypoint** here.

Looks like it's time to heal another Rift and - finally - gain access to that membership card we need!

# STILLED BLOSSU'S HOUSE

There's a total of **five** energy orbs to find here. So, let's get to it.

## Energy Orb 1

Head North, clear out the enemies and set the web on fire for this Energy Orb.

## Energy Orb 2

The second Orb is hidden in the alcove by the Dark Echo plant. Use an aerial Echo or fire to reach it.

## Energy Orb 3

This one is in-between two Deku Baba Lv. 2 plants on the left. Pull their heads off to reach it easily.

## Energy Orb 4

Climb up the first wall, go to the far right, fly across, then burn the web on the ground for the fourth Energy Orb.

## Energy Orb 5

Go to the top level on the left, go in the cave, then bomb the sparkling blocks at the top for the fifth and final Energy Orb.

Tri gains more power and you get an extra **2 x** [Might Crystals] for all your effort.

128/150 Collected! ■

## Prison Break (Again)

Well, *that* didn't quite go as expected!... No matter, we've broken out of jail once already!

Alright, use Bind to pull the cell key to you to unlock the door. Head down the left-hand set of stairs and it's time to get sneaky!

Go through the middle box and pots to go unseen.

Wait for the next Deku to turn to face the other way before moving around it in two moves.

The pair of Deku Scrubs up next need to be facing up/down first (now move down), then facing right/left (to pass them unseen at the bottom).

In the next room, you can pull the trees closer to the exit and the central cell to act as stepping stones.

However, you'll also need to use the bed in the cell to act as a bridge for getting over the gap where the table is.

Drag the table across with Bind, stack it on the top of the bed, and lift them both to the cell wall/bars. Now use all of these items as a platform for jumping across to the exit on the right.

Hit the switch in the next room, but come back to the room on the left, and enter the doorway you opened by moving the plants.

Use a Platboom to reach the [Piece of Heart] at the top.

♥ 34/40 Collected? ☐

Exit the room, go right, then up, then right, and spawn your biggest Echo and carry it through the room to scare all of the Deku Scrubs!

Use another Platboom to make it up past the left-hand water jets to the ladder at the top.

Once you've escaped, you're *finally* given the **[Membership Card]**! Immediately make a beeline for the closed door so we can make use of this card!

Once you're in there, clear out the Dark Echoes that come looking for a fight and get ready to enter the main Rift that leads to this areas dungeon!

Go down the well in the next room, swim through with your Lizalfos Lv. 3 to hand and then use a Tile to fly over the water jets section.

Swim to the far right, move the Boulders back to the left, and use a Platboom to reach the [Might Crystal] that's in the water.

128/150 Collected!

# STILLED FARON WETLANDS

Take the Northern path and there's a few chest to be had if you stick to the Western side of the map (**20 Rupees** and also **4 x [Fresh Milk]**).

Go to the right and you'll encounter an annoying *Electric Keese* flying around. Use some Arrows to bring it down for learning.

▽ *109/127 Learned!* ☐

Burn the web here too for a chest with a **[Golden Egg]** in it.

Continue North-easterly until you reach the **Waypoint**. Activate it then equip your Wind-cannon.

Stand in the middle of the torches and turn it on while rotating the left-stick 360 degrees, blowing out all the torches at once, opening up the exit in front of you!

Climb up the ladder, then up the climbing wall, in the next room, use your Spark Echo to hit all **three green switches**. Continue North to enter the main dungeon!

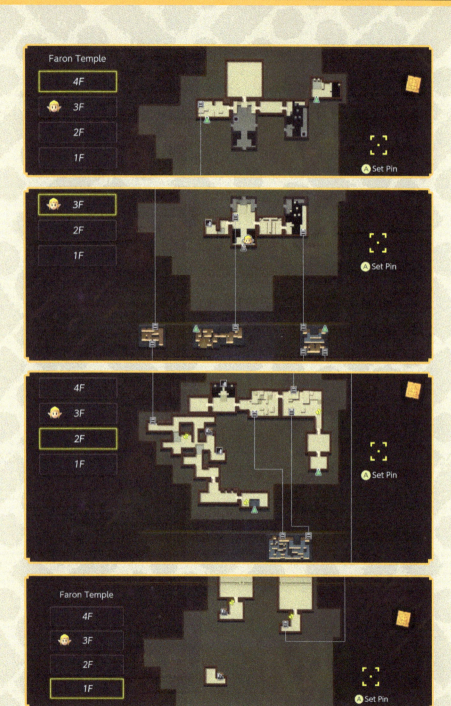

*Caution!* *This* *is* *the* *longest* *dungeon you'll have faced so far! There's four floors and a lot of going in and out of the dungeon and the Still world. Keep this in mind as you're playing!*

Activate the **Waypoint**, go back outside, and use a Platboom to reach the the roof.

Head to the right and move out the second statue with Bind to reveal a hidden doorway.

In this room, use an extended Spark Echo in the middle of the two green gems, and then do the same, but at an angle for the third.

Take the **[Small Key]** from the chest, head back outside, run to the far left, drop down, and go down the ladder here.

You can use an extended Bind on the chest to push it off if you want the **10 x [Warm Peppers]** inside of it.

Exit the room, go back up to the temple roof on the right, and enter the doorway on your left.

Skip the enemies in this room by running to the right, and then use the Small Key on the door here.

## Boss-Fight Warm-Up

This isn't a full boss fight, so don't worry. However, the strategy you use here will work equally well when you actually face off against it a little bit later for real.

Bring out your strongest close-range Echo (we used our *Darknut Lv. 3*, but even the *Lizalfos Lv. 3* will work well if you rapidly keep spawning it in during battle).

Focus on pulling one of the two heads as far back as you can, so your Echo can attack it much more easily.

As soon as you've damaged both heads enough, it'll go underground (for now).

Exit the room, then stand on the switch to drop the metal barrier down.

Go through the right-hand door, and quickly jump across the barriers to the other side.

In this puzzle room, if you want **50 Rupees**, go down the ladder, then open the chest in the water.

Otherwise, go up to the end of the room, use a Platboom to reach the upper level, and use extended Spark Echo shots to hit all three green crystals, opening the door.

Grab the **[Dungeon Map]** from the chest, hit the switch here, go through the door in the bottom-left corner (near the ladder), run through the door that's hidden by the tall grass on the left, save your game (as you're about to use what may be your only Radiant Potion)!

## Glow-up

With the game manually saved, drink the **Radiant Potion** we said to make earlier on as this gives you **5 minutes** of seeing much more easily in the dark.

Go down, pull the Deku Baba's head, then light the torch by the locked door.

Go up and left, and activate the **Waypoint** here. Go right and then immediately up, light the two torches here as well.

From here, head to the far left and go up the ladder.

At the top, use a *Ghini* Ghost to hit the switch on the other side. Climb up and open the chest for a **[Small Key]**.

Go back down, past the Waypoint, and go back to the locked door you lit the torch beside a little earlier.

Grab the **[Golden Egg]** from the chest in the room, head around to the left (and then down), past the moving spikes, until you enter a room where the door locks behind you.

The trick here is to briefly touch the statue on the right and quickly run to the orange tile and stand on it *at the exact same time* as the statue!

This opens up both doors in this room. Go right, activate the **Waypoint**, then dive down into the water, taking you back out into the Stilled world.

Go right, then up, and burn the small spider's web here, that's hiding an entrance.

Just like last time, we need to touch the tile at the same time as the statue.

So, move the bottom one to the left, look up, and then spawn in your own Echo version and time it so you both step on the tiles together, opening up the door to the next room.

In this room, hold the Electric Wizzrobe as long as you can with Bind, while you use your strongest aerial Echo to take it out. This may take a few goes to do though.

Activate the next **Waypoint** and then head up, light the torch, then

go left and light up all remaining unlit torches in this room. Once you've done that, burn the spider's web on the ground that's covering a ladder down.

Add the *Zora's Scale* to your active accessory list as you'll need the air for this one!

What we found worked best for us, was to drop a couple of Boulders under the water jet platform, spawn in a statue, activate it, and then Reverse Bond to it to have it drag you through the current as it moves right-to-left.

If you want to grab the chest on the left, it's got **50 Rupees** in it.

Climb the ladder and then, in the next room, run around lighting up all the unlit torches (as your 'Glow Timer' has likely almost ran out - if it hasn't already).

Light up all three green gems in here with Sparks and go left.

Break the stripped eggs with your sword for heart pieces, go up the stairs, and then you need to solve a counter-weight puzzle.

Remove the rock from the left-hand platform and look up at the switch ahead of you. Send a statue up, run to the right, then synchronize stepping on the switches together to open the door.

Go down through the bottom-left door and grab the **[Small Key]** from the chest in here.

Go right (through three rooms) and use a Boulder in here to jump up to the ladder quickly.

Go down the ladder, use the **Waypoint** and get ready for the proper mini-boss fight!

## BOSS FIGHT: MANHANDLA

This can be a *super* quick and easy fight if you go in with a solid close-quarter *Echo* (we used the *Darknut Lv. 3 Echo*, but another hard-hitting Echo will do).

The trick here is to use **Bind** to pull at each Deku head until it comes off. However, don't expect them to just pop off immediately. It'll take a few goes to take even one off.

Hopefully, your Echo will be fighting your corner with the other heads, but be ready to recast your Echo if need be.

As long as you stay away and use an **extended bind** to pull at the heads, this battle will be over in no time at all.

Once it's dead, grab the **[Big Key]** from the chest. Leave the room, go back up the ladder, and make your way back to the room with the red counter weights. Go through that door, activate the **Waypoint** and get ready to face off against the dungeon's final boss!

 ## BOSS FIGHT: GOHMA

### 1st Phase

Bring in some *Platboom* Echoes to this fight as they'll help quickly dispatch of the bosses eggs later on.

Begin by staying back and dodging the webs on the ground, Get up close to the boss and use the *Platboom* on the eggs.

Bring out your strongest flying Echo, dodge the laser beam attack, and then when the boss hits the ground, jump on top of it and unleash your strongest close-range Echo on it while using your sword.

### 2nd Phase

Switch to the *Spark* Echo now, and lure the boss into a corner. Fire off a few Sparks and you want them to hit the **3 crystals** located on its legs. Once all three at lit up, the boss drops back down to the ground and is open to attack!

### 3rd Phase

The boss repeats all of phase 1 and 2's attacks, but ups the speed and how many eggs and webs it drops on the ground.

Bust out the *Platboom* Echoes and your best aerial Echo to take out its eye when it opens.

When it falls, get back on top of it and use your best close-range Echo and your sword to end this fight.

# RIFT ON HOLY MOUNT LANAYRU

 **It'll be Ice to See You at the Summit**

With Tri now stronger (reaching Level 9 with us, granting us one more cast), you're given another **5 x [Might Crystals]**.

As soon as you regain control of Zelda, head South and speak with the Deku Scrub on the left with the red exclamation mark to start the *Cotton-Candy Hunt* Side Quest.

## Going for 100%

Go South-west and pull the Scrub out from the ground to start the *Mobbing Mothulas* Side Quest.

Now go speak with the Scrubs just to the East and you'll trigger the *Looking for Bempu* Side Quest.

Continue Eastward to the Smoothie Shop, and speak with the Scrub outside to start the *Mythical Deku Snake* Side Quest. Give him **three Electro Apples** now to finish Side Quest immediately.

Take your **5 x [Monster Stones]** and then pull *Bempu* out of the ground as he's hiding right outside the Smoothie Shop!

Continue heading South-east, and keep an eye out for the swarm of Mothula's. Take them all out (for the *Mobbing Mothulas* Side Quest), then continue West.

Drop down into the water, kill the two blue *Drippitune* frogs here (to stop it raining), then use a Platboom and some Braziers to light the two torches high up in the water.

Head down the steps into the *Hidden Ruins* (which is actually a mini dungeon with a mini-boss at the end!).

## Hidden Ruins

Open the chest for a **[Monster Stone]**, switch to your Spark Echo, hit the yellow box with it, head right, then set the top right-hand web on fire to reveal the yellow box for this room. This one needs **two Sparks** in it to open the door ahead.

In the next room, use Bind to drag the Boulder up to the side of the yellow box, then face the Boulder and fire off **three Sparks** at it to open the door ahead.

Go down the ladder, then use a Flying Tile to quickly cross the gap (jumping off at the end).

Use Bind to pull the chest above you down to you for **20 Rupees**.

Now use a *Strandtula* to climb up the far right and exit the room.

Jump across the water (using the boxes) and fire down **three Sparks** into the yellow box to open the gate ahead.

Switch to your *Lava Rock* Echo and get ready to face-off against the mini-boss in the next room!

## 1st Phase

Alright, for the rematch, it's time to get a little bit… creative. Select a *Lava Rock* and use this to guide one of the small clouds onto the top of it.

If you follow its speed, then you can guide it to the other cloud(s) moving around!

Once the boss is big again, jump up onto the ledge opposite the purple tiles and use a *Platboom* to drop repeatedly onto the boss' head as it ties to come up at you from both sides (it'll switch direction each time).

## 2nd Phase

While you want to repeat the trick of using *Lava Rock* for "guiding" the mini clouds together, don't forget you can use **Bind** to force them to go in the opposite direction (this is super handy if you can anticipate their paths).

However, the clouds will also fire out some electricity, so don't be afraid to use a Shock Resistant potion/smoothie if it helps.

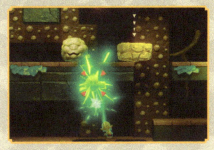

Repeat the process of dropping *Platbooms* on its head and it'll be done for once and for all! Finally!

Be sure to collect the [Piece of Heart] it drops!

35/40 Collected? ■

Alright, with that finished, manually warp to the heart-shaped island Waypoint, head to the top left-hand corner and pull out *Bempu* again.

Now warp to the Waypoint by the Smoothie Shop and head West to speak with the Deku to let it know you've completed the *Cotton-Candy Hunt* Side Quest!

You'll be rewarded with the upgraded **[Curious Charm]** (which reduces the damage you take *even further!*).

Put this accessory on, then head South-west and pull the Scrub back out from the ground.

You'll be rewarded with a **[Might Crystal]** for completing the *Mobbing Mothulas* Side Quest!

Make your way North of the Wetlands prison (go over the trees) and you'll find *Bempu* hiding in the ground in between the four Deku Scrub statue heads.

Now warp to the most South-easterly Waypoint in the Wetlands and pull *Bempu* out of his final hiding spot.

You'll be rewarded with the **[Fairy Fragrance]** accessory for finishing the *Looking for Bempu* Side Quest.

We're done in the Wetlands, so lets head North. Warp to the Waypoint by the *Eternal Forest*.

## Northern Hyrule

Alright, you've done loads already and we're getting closer to the end! However, there's still quite a few Echoes, items, and more to find before we tackle the last boss. We won't be satisfied until you've completed this game 100%!

## Eternal Forest

Once you arrive, immediately head West into the foggy forest. Then go up to activate the **Waypoint**.

Head West from here and take out the strong **Sword Moblin Lv. 3** with your own Lv. 3 Echo!

▼ *110/127 Learned!* ☐

Take the **50 Rupees** from the nearby buried chest, now head down the small grass ramp and look for the **hoove prints** in the dirt.

**Follow their directions** (almost in an anti-clockwise circle) until you reach the large opening where the super-powerful **Lynel** is hiding!

We've got a full page dedicated to it back on page 16.

However, one way is to spam the life out of your Lv. 3 Darknut or the Ball-and-Chain Echoes against it. It'll soon go down if you're relentless. Make sure to learn it as it's **the most powerful Echo in the game**!

▼ *111/127 Learned!* ☐

We're not done here yet though. Use a Platboom to get on top of the trees, and look for the grass with a circle of plants up to the left. There's a [Might Crystal] hidden under the middle bush.

136/150 Collected! ☐

Warp back to the Eternal Forest Waypoint, then go South-east to the Smoothie Shop by the tree.

Mix together a few potions using your **Warm Peppers** (we recommend making a couple of **Warming Potions**, which requires 1 Pepper + 1 Monster Fang each, and a couple of **Golden Piping-Hot Smoothies** (which requires 1 Pepper + 1 Golden Egg each).

## To Hebra Mountain

Alright, where you're going, it's going to get **very chilly**! (Which is why you made those smoothies and potions there now).

Head North from the Smoothie Shop and you'll encounter a blocked door. Blow it up with a bomb and head down the ladder.

Once you enter the cave, go right, use a Tile to cross the gap, and then a *Bombfish* to blow up the blocks (hold it until it starts flashing quickly, *then* throw it).

Jump on the platform, use bombs to clear the path up, head left at the top if you want the **9 x [Warm Peppers]** from the block-covered chest.

Climb up the wall to the top, move the large boulder right with Bind, blow a hole in the cracked blocks, pull the large boulder back over the gap to the left, drop down, and get on the platform heading up.

Go up, then up the ladder, and exit the cave to be on top of the snowy mountain.

## Hebra Mountain

It's going to be getting rather chilly up here soon, but let's start things off by activating the **Waypoint** on the left.

Your *Lynel* will be the main choice of combat Echo moving forwards, so use it on the **Snowmaul** enemy just down the path.

112/127 Learned!

Keep an eye out on the left side for the next **[Stamp Stand]**.

23/25 Located!

Once the blizzard kicks in, it's time to drink one of your **Potions** (save the Golden Smoothies until you *really* need them as they also replenish **all** you energy as well as give you 5 minutes Chill-Proof).

**Top Tip!** *Run out of potions? Carrying a Brazier or an Ignizol with you also works. However, it makes combat **much** harder. So, be careful!*

Follow the Braziers Northward and take out and learn the **Leever** that pops up out of the snow.

113/127 Learned!

When you reach the blocked entrance, use a *Platboom* to reach the ledge above and melt the ice block with fire to reveal a hidden [Might Crystal].

137/150 Collected!

Drop down and melt the ice in front of the cave's entrance, and go inside.

Use a fire-based Echo to melt some of the **Ice Blocks** here and learn its Echo now.

114/127 Learned!

Use a P*latboom* to go up (if you melt all the ice) and the chest contains **8 x [Floral Nectar]**

Drop down, go left, climb up, then use a Ghost to hit the switch through the wall to open the gate. Inside this chest is a **[Golden Egg]**.

Leave the cave using the same way you came in, and if you want them, the buried chest contains **6 x [Twisted Pumpkins]**.

Run back down to the creature laying face down in the snow. Follow him around a couple of corners, but keep an eye out for a ramp going up to the right, near some grass.

Head up here and speak with the *Business Scrub*. Show him a **Twisted Pumpkin** and you'll immediately complete the *Getting it Twisted* Sub Quest!

You'll be rewarded with **10 x [Warm Peppers]** as thanks. Now activate the **Waypoint** just up to its left and exit the way you came.

When you reach the Brazier, head left and look for a new Wolf enemy

in the snow. Take it out and learn the **Wolfos Echo**.

▼ *115/127 Learned!* ☐

Go down, to the long grass, and lift the Boulder up in the middle to reveal a [Might Crystal].

*138/150 Collected!* ☐

Run to the far right to catch up with your new friend. Go up first and use some Arrows on the *Ice Keese*, and learn their Echo.

▼ *116/127 Learned!* ☐

Pull the chest off the ledge for **11 x [Monster Guts]**. Now speak with your friend and activate the next **Waypoint**.

From here, go directly East (ignoring our friend - for now), and follow this path around and up.

Clear out the Lv. 2 Sword Moblins here and melt ALL the ice to reveal a few more hidden away.

Once the coast is clear, climb up for the chest with **10 x [Radiant Butter]** inside.

From here, use a *Platboom* to climb over the top of the trees above you and enter the out-of-sight cave entrance near the Rift's edge.

Clear out the Lv. 3 Moblin here and open the chest for the **[Energy Belt]** accessory.

Go South-west after exiting this cave, over the treetops, and drop down for the hidden **[Stamp Stand]** (one more to go!).

24/25 Located!

From here, go left (over the trees), and look for an ice block on its own by the cliff edge close by.

Melt this and claim the **[Might Crystal]** hidden inside the ice.

139/150 Collected!

Drop down and speak with *Condé*. Once the cut-scene has ended, head inside the cave and melt the ice in the top right-hand corner of the room.

Jump over the ice blocks to the exit, then you can use Bind to bring the chest up above you down to you (avoiding the Snowballs) for **50 Rupees**.

Go back into the ice block room and melt the ice in the top left-hand corner to reveal the doorway.

Melt the ice block on the left and get ready to enter the Rift here.

There's a total of **five** energy orbs to find here. So, let's get to it.

## Energy Orb 1

From the start go to the left-hand edge, fly South-west and the Orb is in ice on the Island with grass.

## Energy Orb 2

Fly North and clear out the enemies before melting the ice in the middle for the Energy Orb.

## Energy Orb 3

From here, go North, then fly North-east. The Orb is on a ledge, waiting to be collected.

## Energy Orb 4

Fly back the way you came, head then use a *Platboom* to go straight up to the ledge holding the Orb and a Dark Echo.

## Energy Orb 5

Go West slightly, then look down and drop a fire-type Echo on the ice to melt it. Drop down onto the Energy Orb to grab the last one!

Tri gains more power and you get an extra **2 x** [Might Crystals] for all your effort.

**141/150 Collected!**

Once you're back on the mountain, head up the ladder, and use your fire-echoes to clear a path through the ice blocks.

Quickly dash under the *Snowball* that drops down here, catch it with Bind and learn it now.

▼ 117/127 *Learned!* ☐

Climb up the ladder and wall and there's a chest on the left if you want the **[Monster Stone]** in it.

Exit the cave and activate the **Waypoint** outside. Use a *Platboom* up the right-hand cliff and get the **[Piece of Heart]**.

♥ 36/40 *Collected?* ☐

Drop down to the icy water on the right and use some Arrows to quickly kill the *Ice Wizzrobe* here for its Echo.

▼ 118/127 *Learned!* ☐

There's also a chest in the water you can pull out with **20 Rupees** in it.

West from here is a larger pool of water. Use your *Tiles* and *Platbooms* to reach the **[Piece of Heart]** up on the platform by the trees.

♥ 37/40 *Collected?* ☐

From here, use a Tile to fly to the left (cross the clouds below) and you'll reach a snowy cave entrance. Head inside, and then take care of and learn the *Tektite Lv. 2*.

▼ 119/127 *Learned!* ☐

Go into the next room and clear it out, making sure to learn the *Ice Octo Echo*.

▼ 120/127 *Learned!* ☐

Once learned, go open the chest that appears for the **[Ice Spike]** accessory (stops you slipping on ice when wearing them).

Put them on for here (along with the Golden Sash if you have it), head outside, and melt the ice in the middle of the grass a bit for a [Might Crystal].

142/150 Collected!

Now fly right again (over the clouds below), and head up into the cave.

Use a *Platboom* to go up, and (if you have the spikes and sash equipped), you can simply walk through this room. Otherwise, use Bind to lift up and drop the Wind-cannons into the abyss below.

Go through the door at the top of the room, clear the ice block room of enemies (melt the top right-hand corner ice block for a hidden enemy), and go through the left-hand door.

Melt the ice and open the chest for **6 x [Monster Guts]**.

Go back into the ice block room, then go up. In this room, use your Lynel/strongest Echo on the **Freezards**.

▼ 121/127 Learned! ☐

Dash through the next few rooms and then be careful of the light-blue icicles, as they constantly fall, re-grow, and fall.

Time your movements very carefully, and use Bind to pull the *Ice Octos* off their platforms.

When heading up the platform, use a statue at either side of you to block you from the icy winds.

Once you exit the tunnel and are back outside, head left and then watch out for the new flying-eye enemy, the **Moa**. Take one down and learn it.

▽ **122/127 Learned!** ☐

### Snowball Valley

Be super careful of all the large Snowballs that will be rolling down from up above! You *can* use Bind to hold a *Boulder* out in front of you as a shield (it won't protect you from all angles though).

Jump or fly across to the [Piece of Heart] that's sitting openly on the snow-covered island.

♥ **38/40 Collected?** ☐

As you head around the narrow, snow-covered trail, keep an eye out for some ice on the edge of the trail. Melt it and a [Might Crystal] appears.

◈ **143/150 Collected!** ☐

Once you reach Condé at the top, activate the nearby **Waypoint**. Jump up and then proceed to head in a North-easterly direction. Speak with *Stamp Guy* to start the *Stamp Stand Swallowed!* Side Quest.

## STILLED HEBRA MOUNTAIN PASSAGE

There's a total of **three** energy orbs to find here. So, let's get to it.

## Energy Orb 1

From the start, make your way across to the far left-side of the map. Melt the ice to make the Energy Orb appear.

## Energy Orb 2

Head right (back to the entrance), then continue over to the right-hand side of the map. On the far right-hand side are more ice blocks. Kill the *Dark Freezard* that's here to unlock access to the Energy Orb.

## Energy Orb 3

Go back to the entrance and then head directly up. You can safely swim in this water, but we recommend you step out half-way up and use a *Platboom* to get up to the top and then melt the ice *from above* using a few *Ignizols*.

Collect the final Energy Orb here to complete this smaller Rift.

Tri gains more power and you get an extra **2 x** [Might Crystals] for all your effort.

145/150 Collected!

If you've unlocked Level 10 for Tri now (which we did), you can also cast a few more Echoes for less.

With the Rift closed, you'll complete the *Stamp Stand Swallowed!* Side Quest, earning you a little dance.

However, if this also happens to be the last **[Stamp Stand]** to find on your adventure, then you'll be rewarded with the **[Stamp Suit]** for your efforts!

25/25 Located!

With the suit now in your possession, head in a North-westerly direction, past all the rolling Snowballs, and keep an eye out for chests along the way.

Look at the map for the large Rift and to the South-west of it there'll be an entrance with a ladder leading up. Go inside.

Make your way up and through the cave (using *Boulders* as shields from the Snowballs), and continue up.

When you see the green hot spring, use your strongest Echo on the two **Temper Tweelus** enemies.

123/127 Learned!

Head outside, activate the **Waypoint** up here,

Speak with Conde and you'll now need to enter the Rift that leads to this area's dungeon (the final one of the three needed).

You ready? Let's get to it.

# STILLED HEBRA MOUNTAIN

From the start, heard Northward and follow the path around to the left. Jump across to where the chest is, and you can now learn the *Cloud Echo*.

▼ 124/127 Learned!

These can be stacked on top of each other and used as more effective platforms. Grab the [Monster Stone] from the chest, then fly up North and enter the doorway that's at the top.

*Platbooms* and *Tiles* are super useful in the side-on part for navigating between all of the clouds (it feels like a proper platformer at this part!).

Keep heading right, climb up the walls (being careful of the *Freeze Slugs*, grab their Echo, then head up the ladder.

▼ 125/127 Learned!

Exit the cave, then go North-east to reach the Dungeon's entrance.

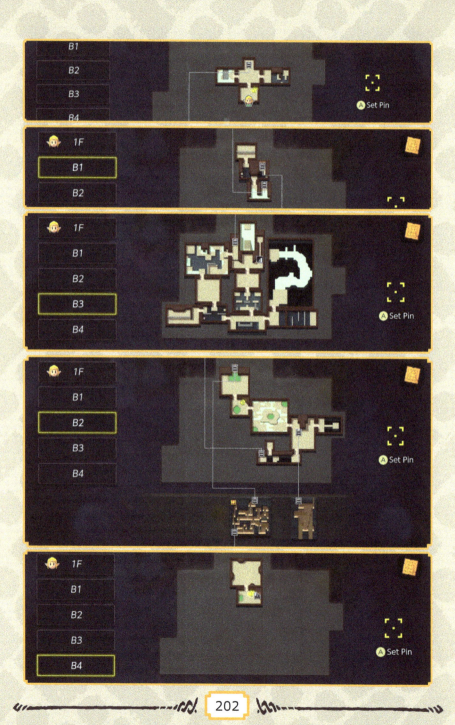

B1
B2
B3
B4

A Set Pin

1F
B1
B2

1F
B1
B2
B3
B4

A Set Pin

1F
B1
B2
B3
B4

A Set Pin

1F
B1
B2
B3
B4

A Set Pin

As always, activate the **Waypoint** when you enter.

In the left-hand door, clear out the enemies for the chest to appear. Inside are **5 x [Rock Salt]**.

Go through the right-hand door and then fly over to the red orb, The goal is to put it in the other pedestal to activate the heating fan (melting the ice in that room).

Fly back on a Tile with it and drop it in the pedestal to activate it.

Head down the ladder, you can use Bind to drag the chest with **3 x [Monster Fangs]** to you, then head down the ladder.

In the next two rooms, use *Boulders* to block off the jets of icy-cold wind. Head up into the top-left corner door, block off the Icy-wind here and use Bind to drop the red ball onto the other pedestal to activate the heat fan.

In the previous room, swim down into the water and pick up the - easy to miss - **[Small Key]**.

If you go *back* into the room with the red orb in it, dropping it *back onto the same pedestal* actually turns it blue, re-freezing the water!

To get past the Icy-jets in the previous room (to reach the doorway), use some *Boulders* and *Statues* to block them and create some steps up.

In the side-on cave, use Bind to carry a statue to your side to protect you as you climb up and down the wall.

Be extra careful of the Icicles dropping around you (although, you *can* use Bind to pick them off and also use *those* as shields!). HA!

In the next room, if you use a *platboom* to go up by the Ice-jet, then you can reach a secret room that holds a chest with a **[Golden Egg]** inside!

From this high-up platform, use a *Tile* to fly right across to the door on the right!

In the next room, melt the top-right ice block to reveal a ladder.

Carefully climb down the wall, and use Bind to bring the red crystal up. You can use a *Statue* to stick to the left-side of the cave (avoiding the Ice-jets on the right).

Drop it in the pedestal in the top right-hand corner of the cave and the room above will be heated up.

Go through the right-hand door and push the ice block over to the pressure pad and stand on the one below you at the same time to reveal the room's chest.

Take the **[Small Key]** from it and then clear the next room of the *Temper Tweelus* enemies. Grab the **[Dungeon Map]** from the chest that appears.]

In the next room, be sure to activate the **Waypoint** as you're about to face-off against this dungeon's mini-boss!

This mini-boss is a battle of attrition. It's super weak to being frozen, so we **strongly** recommend that you bring some *Ice Octos* to the party.

Hold the boss in place with **Bind** and press **Y** to drop a couple of *Ice Octos* beside it to freeze it. Now use your sword to hack away at it whilst it's frozen.

However, Link's Awakening players will feel a sense of Deja-vu when the boss begins to split up!

Be super careful when you see one of the halves jumping up into the air! Keep an eye on the ground for its shadow and be ready to move!

Be mindful of the bits of the boss going for a dip in the hot spring water! They'll even shoot a stream of hot water at its buddies that are frozen to defrost them quicker!

Keep locking on and placing out as many *Ice Octos* as you can, while constantly switching in and out of *Swordfighter* mode to deal damage to all frozen blobs.

If you keep it up long enough, all of the smallest blobs will be frozen and you'll emerge victorious!

Head down the ladder and in the next cave-area, you need to make sure **all** of the torches are lit.

Start by melting the ice on the left, then light that torch. Now go right, and use an extended cast Brazier echo on the torch up here (or drag one up from below, your choice).

Before exiting this room, use a *Water Block* on top of the Brazier here and swim up to the top. There's a chest up here with a handy **100 Rupees** in it!

There's quite a few things we need to do to gain access to the Big Key.

## Operation Big Key

In the room with the Big Key, drop down, head down, ignore the blue crystal and continue down into the next room.

Use a *Tile* on the left to skip half the room, melt the ice, but claim the **3 x [Twisted Pumpkins]** from the chest before going down.

In the next room just go right, then up, and you'll be in a large room with a red crystal.

If you have the *Ice Spikes* and *Golden Sash* here, then you can easily walk around the room.

Otherwise, you'll need to send out your strongest Echo and then use Bind to - slowly - carry the red crystal to the pedestal at the top of the room.

Once the ice has been melted in the other rooms, fly back down towards the door, go through, and - if you want the **[Monster Stone]** in the chest in this room - start swimming in the water to the right.

Don't forget that you can actually drag the Tektite Lv. 2's down into the water to get rid of them.

After emptying the chest, go left, dive into the water and place a *Boulder* on the switch down here, opening up the door on the left.

In the next room, go straight through the door in the top left-hand corner, place a boulder in front of each of the wind jets, but leave the icy-jet alone.

Carry the red crystal through it (with Bind) and watch how the icy blast turns the crystal blue!

Go back into the previous room, place an *Ice Block* down in front of the pressure pad at the other side of the room, push the ice so it slides over to the pressure plate, jump over the bar, and step on the pressure pad down here **at the same time as the ice block does!** This opens the door at the top.

In the next room, use your strongest Echo and Swordfighter form to clear it out of the **White Wolfos** that are in here.

▼ *126/127 Learned!* ☐

In the next room, be careful to clear out the *Freezards* here as they can be a real pain. Use extended casts and your strongest Echoes to take them out from a distance.

The easy way to carry the red crystal to the pedestal in this room is to go wait for the first icy blast to stop, then push the ice block on the right into the water, using it to cross.

Go up the ladder, hit the switch, leave the room and you'll be back in the room with the Big Key in it.

Go down once again, and then **light the torch here and use it to change the crystal's color!**

Very sneaky eh?! Now drop the red crystal into the pedestal on the left to melt the ice that's blocking the big yellow button that unlocks access to the Big Key.

However, we're not *quite* finished yet. Take the crystal (that's turned blue again) and place *that* on the left-hand pedestal as well to re-freeze the water to the button (otherwise, the snowball sinks in the water).

Go up, stand on the switch, and then go claim your - well deserved- **[Big Key]**!

There's a hidden **20 Rupee** coin located right above the doorway that leads down. Use a *platboom* to get up high enough to reach it.

Go down the steps, activate the **Waypoint** down here, and if you need a health top-up, simply stand in the hot spring water on the left before opening the door to this dungeon's boss.

# BOSS FIGHT: SKORCHILL

## 1st Phase

This can be a tough fight, so make sure to bring some **Fire** and **Ice** Echoes (preferably *Wizzrobes*), a hard-hitting Lv. 3 Echo for close-up hits, and put on the **Ice Spikes** as they'll help *a lot* for a later phase.

This time, the helmet requires **three** direct hits to break it. Switch back to your close-range Echo to hit it hard while you distract it by locking on and moving around the room.

The first goal is to use a fire-based attack to destroy the boss' helmet. If you can be the bait, then it gives your Echo a better chance of landing successful hits.

After **two** helmet hits, it's time to switch up to close-attacks. This is where your strongest Echo comes in. Feel free to fire off some Arrows or throw bombs at the boss as well as it'll try and stomp you if you get too close.

## 3rd Phase

Switch back to a **Fire-based** Echo to get rid of the horns on the helmet. **Three** hits are needed, then one final all-out assault with a close-range Echo and your *Swordfighter* form will finish this fight.

## 2nd Phase

It's time to switch it up to an ice-based Echo. Once again, be the bait, while dodging the fire attacks.

Once you've cleared this area of the Rift, you'll be rewarded with the final **5 x** [Might Crystals] and - if you max out Tri at Level 11 - then the cost to reduce some of the best Echoes is reduced by one!

150/150 Collected! ■

## RESCUING THE HERO LINK

◀•◆•▶ **You're on the Final Stretch, Let's Go!** ◀•◆•▶

While we *could* go and finish the game now, we're going to make sure we get all remaining items and Echoes for those of you who are as keen to get 100% as we were.

### The Prime Energy and Null

Once the cut-scenes have all ended, warp to the Southern Waypoint on *Hebra Mountain*.

Head to *Condé's* house and speak with *Condé* to start the *Snowball Magic* Side Quest.

The trick to success here is to grab the Snowball with Bind and then use a *Boulder* to smash the

snowballs that come down the hill at you. Keep this up until you reach the top where you need to place the Snowball down.

Your rewards is a [Piece of Heart]. Only one more to go!

39/40 Collected? ■

Now warp all the way down to *Luberry's* house. Upgrade the Bombs to Level 2.

If you've been following our guide closely, then offer Luberry a further **25 Might Crystals** and he creates a pot outside of his house that you can visit at any time and it'll **refill all of your Swordfighter energy bar as often as you like!**

If you've fully upgraded your Swordfighter form, you'll also notice that your sword also fires a projectile that damages enemies!

## Final 100% Sweep

Make your way to *Suthorn Village* and speak with the young boy there. Show him a *Snowball* to complete the *What Is Snow… Really?* Side Quest.

After taking the **8 x [Floral Nectar]**, warp to *Kakariko Village*.

Go inside the *Slumber Dojo* and the remaining challenges will now be unlocked. As before, please head to page 244 for the our tips on how to beat each of them.

If you do the remaining challenges now, you'll earn the following rewards:

- *3 x Monster Stones*
- *7 x Rocktatoes (speed bonus)*
- *8 x Monster Guts*
- *7 x Electro Apples (Speed Bonus)*
- **[Second Mastery Accessory]**
- *8 x Radiant Butter*
- *7 x Twisted Pumpkins (speed bonus)*
- *8 x Twisted Pumpkins*
- *7 x Chilly Cactus (speed bonus)*
- *3 x Golden Eggs*
- *7 x Monster Fangs (speed bonus)*
- *[(Final) Piece of Heart]!*
- *5 x Golden Eggs*
- *7 x Rock Salt (speed bonus)*
- *50 Rupees*
- *7 x Monster Guts (speed bonus)*
- *5 x Monster Stones*
- *7 x Fresh Milk*
- **[Final Mastery]!**
- **The Green Tunic (Link's Clothes)!**

Phew! That was **a lot** of work, but the rewards were *well* worth it!

> **Top Tip!** *You can actually equip every mastery scroll and their effects stack on top of each other!* **Very** *handy for super long boss fights…*

Just note that you can only hold **20 smoothies** at any one time. So, you can simply sell 10 of them back to the Business Scrub to free up space and use those Rupees to make the final 10 recipes needed.

You'll be rewarded with the **[Survey Binoculars]** for completing this Side Quest.

If you stick around and finish making **every single smoothie and potion** (again, see our complete list near the start of the guide for the ingredients needed), then you'll be rewarded with **10 x [Golden Eggs]**.

| | |
| --- | --- |
| 🛡 Damage Reduced + | |
| 🔋 ⟨ Energy Consumption Reduced Lv. 2 | |
| 🔋 ⟨ Energy Consumption Reduced Lv. 1 | |
| 🔋 ⟨ Energy Consumption Reduced Lv. 3 | |

Business Scrub

*Incredible that we've finally documented all the ways you can blend food with other food!*

Leave the Dojo and, head South to the *Smoothie Shop* and let's go bonkers making **30 Smoothie Recipes** for the *Recipes, Please!* Side Quest (You should have *loads* of ingredients by now).

Head to page 18 for the full list of what you can make.

## The Final Challenge

Alright, warp to the *Eternal Forest* and head up to progress the story forwards.

Be sure to learn the **Ancient Orb Echo** while you're here.

▼ 127/127 Learned! ☐

The goal is to now find all **Six Ancient Orb** pedestals and spawn an *Orb* on top of each one to open the way forward.

After placing the first one on the pedestal right in front of the gate, you need to find the remaining five.

## Pedestal 2

Head South-east and then directly South of the Waypoint for the first pedestal.

## Pedestal 3

Travel in a South-easterly direction from here (go over the trees if you like) and it's tucked away near one of the larger trees.

## Pedestal 4

This pedestal can be found if you travel West from the previous pedestal 3. Also near a large tree (but it's more in the open).

## Pedestal 5

From the fourth pedestal, continue traveling West, and when you reach the Snakes and Moblins, the Pedestal is tucked away in the corner, surrounded by four trees.

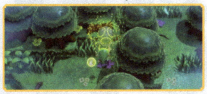

## Pedestal 6

The final pedestal is hiding where the *Deku Baba* is. Pull its head off, then place the Orb on it to unlock the way forward.

Once you arrive in the Stilled Ancient Ruins, use your *Flying Tile* and *Platboom* Echoes to travel directly North.

Travel in a North-westerly direction once you see the boats on the left.

Continue upwards, activate the **Waypoint** here, and the use a *Tile* to fly up (with the freezing water under you) and when you fall into the water, spawn in a *Platboom* to skip all the ice enemies on the left!

Continue Northwards (the *Platboom* will allow you to skip traveling Eastward at all, just use it to keep going up), and activate the next **Waypoint** here when you reach it. **Save your game too!**

It's time for a boss fight…

### 1st Phase

Hopefully you'll have been going after a 100% save file as the extra health and energy bar will prove to be super useful here.

Pull out your strongest ranged Echo, lock on to Dark Zelda, and use charged **Bow** shots while your circle around the arena.

It'll take a few hits before she'll drop down to the ground, which is when she's vulnerable to ground-based attacks/Echoes.

### 2nd Phase

Dark Zelda will now start using stronger ground-based Echoes to attack you with. Bring out your strongest close-range Echo (we used the formidable *Lynel*).

Once again, keep your distance, lock-on to her, and use as many charged Bow shots as you can to bring her down to the ground, where the *real* damage can occur.

### 3rd Phase

Dark Zelda will now bring out her strongest Echoes (thankfully, not her own *Lynel)!*

Keep up the charged bow shots on Dark Zelda while your own Echo deals with the ground-based Echoes coming after you.

You just need to be paying attention as every enemy is moving *much* faster than before, so you need to keep dodging and firing arrows.

Don't be afraid to drink a few smoothies here if required.

Now that you've rescued Link, it's time to make our way to the final boss battle of the game!

There's still a few more enemies to fight and puzzles to solve however, so it won't be plain sailing.

We recommend that you go into your accessory slot and equip the following accessories now:

- *Frog Ring*
- *Ancient Charm*
- *Zora Flippers*
- *Zora Scale*
- *Golden Sash*

## Null's Body

As you follow Link around the first couple of rooms, it's worth noting that Link is both **invincible** *and* he also has **infinite arrows**.

Combine this with your strongest Echo (hopefully the Lynel as it's awesome here), then you can focus on letting the AI do most of the work.

Once you reach the first room of enemies, spawn your Echo and circle the room, letting Link and your Echo take the Dark Echoes on.

In the next room, split up, go right, then use an extended cast of a locked-on *Ghini* to hit the switch in the corner of the room from where you are.

Go down the ladder, then use Reverse Bond on the platforms, making sure to time the second platform (that goes up and down), so that the platform below it (going left to right), allows you to use both to reach the left-hand side of the screen.

Use two *Flying Tiles* in the next area, then a *Platboom* to head up (this is why you put on the *Gold Sash*).

In the next room, stack some *Boulders* up against the right-hand side of the upper platform and then grab Link with Bind and lift him up higher with you, effectively helping him up to the higher platform (without waiting for the AI to figure it out).

We're not gonna lie. This battle is a **very** long, multi-phase battle, so it's *critical* that you have every smoothie slot stacked out with health, energy replenishing (ideally of the golden variety) and damage reduction smoothies! (Seriously).

## 1st Phase

Thankfully, Link is AI controlled and is also invincible! So, we need to help Link by using **Bind** on each arm, while pulling it back, allowing Link to perform a spin attack, severing each of the three arms.

Once every arm is gone, rush in and hit it with your hardest Echo and your sword.

## 2nd Phase

It's important to keep pulling at Null's arms as they come through the wall, but you now need to be extra careful of the dark hands that shoot off when he re-enters the arena again.

Make sure to dodge them as you keep focusing on pulling Null's arms back for Link to sever.

Once again, lay into Null once it hits the ground to move the battle on.

## 3rd Phase

Not only is this a *much* faster version of the previous phase, but Null now also conjures up a large patch of dark energy on the ground that you **must** dodge, or it'll cause *severe* damage!

Keep up the pressure to move the battle to phase four...

## Phase 4

Now you're swimming in side-on view, so immediately put on your **Zora Scale** and **Zora Flippers** if you have them!

You'll want to use your strongest underwater Echo to attack the tentacles (we used a *Lizalflos Lv. 3*) and keep spin swimming up close to Null while repeatedly spamming the **Y** button as the *Lizalflos* sinks to the ground (while causing good damage on the way down).

## Phase 5

Null's not messing around anymore and he's determined to bring the big guns out now!

Bring out your strongest close-range Echo (we used the *Lynel* once again) and resume pulling out the limbs while Link hacks away at them.

Once you deal enough damage, you'll need to dodge the large whirlpools coming at you!

Dash swim back up to Null and keep using your Echoes on the tentacles and Null until you trigger the next phase of the fight.

Be careful though, as Null will start to morph into any one of the previous major bosses, so you need to be ready to dodge their attacks at any point!

Let your Echo focus on attacking Null directly, while you focus solely on pulling off each of Null's arms.

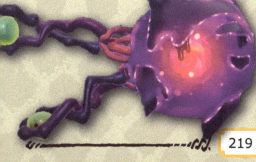

## Phase 6

Summon a couple of Lv. 2 *Sword Moblins* as Null will start dropping off multiple Dark Echoes while sticking his arms out of the wall. Use them as a distraction while you focus on pulling and severing each arm once again.

It's worth keeping a boulder or similar handy in the menu, as they can often be used to deflect the Dark boss form's attacks, saving you from taking damage!

Keep recasting your strongest Echo, keep pulling at Null's arms, and keep dodging the numerous boss forms until you begin phase seven.

## Phase 7

Bust out as many distraction Echoes as you can as Null will start sending out up to **five** Dark Echoes, while also now trying to grab you from the floor!

You really need to be paying extra attention here as it's going to be manic!

Don't be shy with using any damage reduction smoothies here either as this is the last phase of the fight!

Null will now begin to bring in *multiple* different boss Echoes and things **will** be hectic as you'll need to contend with *both* forms of attacks while still focusing on pulling on Null's arm for Link to hack off with his trusty spin attack.

Once you've pulled off the final arm for the final time, a few good hits will see Null hit the ground. Use **Bind** and pull the *Triforce* out of Null to finish the game!

### CONGRATULATIONS!

Now sit back, and enjoy that - well earned - cinematic ending!

# SIDE-QUESTS

## Extra adventures on the side

Side Adventures are new to the 2D games and they're optional missions that often flesh out key character backstories, and they sometimes offer decent rewards for completing them (but, it's mainly rupees and materials used for smoothies that's your reward for completing them).

### Finding the Flying Plant
**Location: Suthorn Village**
**Reward: Might Crystal**

The goal here is to unlock the *Peahat* Echo. The closest one is found in the *Suthorn Forest Cave* (has two - very helpful - fiery *Braziers* that you **should** clone…).

Kill the Peahat with fire, capture the Echo, then show this Echo to the elderly man to complete it.

So I go on a little walk, and what do I find? A giant plant that flies!

### Up a Wall
**Location: Suthorn Prairie**
**Reward: 20 Rupees**

There are so many monsters here. Fight them off for me, please!

The goal here is to clear the two *Spear Moblins* surrounding the man. Use your best Echo(es) here to dispatch them.

He'll thank you for your help and put **20 Rupees** into your pockets. Better than nothing we suppose.

## The Blocked Road

*Location: Suthorn Prairie*
*Reward: 20 Rupees*

You'll come across this guy to the far West of the *Suthorn Prairie*. One solution for clearing the path ahead is to burn the crates with wood.

Alternatively, just lift the items out of the way with **Bind** (easiest). He'll thank you with **20 Rupees**.

## The Flying Tile

*Location: Oasis (Gerudo Desert)*
*Reward: 50 Rupees*

You'll find the *Flying Tiles* hidden away in a cave in the top-left corner of the desert (surrounded by *Boarblin Camps*).

Record the Echo *before* all of the tiles all rise up and destroy themselves and show it to *Tormali* for a reasonable **50 Rupees**.

## Elusive Tumbleweeds

*Location: Gerudo Town*
*Reward: 2 x Might Crystals*

This can be surprisingly frustrating as a captured *Tumbleweed* can be **very** fragile! There's one blowing around South-West of the Gerudo's location.

Capture it with a **short** Bind (keeping it close) and *very carefully* walk back to the Gerudo with it for **Two Might Crystals**!

## Beetle Ballyhoo

Location: Gerudo Town
Reward: Heart Barrette

**After c**ompleting the *Still Missing* main quest, speak to this Gerudo. You need to clear out the **four Beetle Mounds** hidden inside the Northern cave, found at the top-center of the desert. After claiming the echo, destroy the mounds and speak with her for the **[Heart Barrette]**!

## Gerudo Tag Training

Location: Gerudo Town
Reward: 6 x Chilly Cactus

Your supposed to block her path with Echoes in an effort to slow her down as you try and catch her.

Honestly, it's quicker to just keep spinning as you follow her and you'll catch her quicker than you think! She'll give you **Six [Chilly Cactus]** for your troubles.

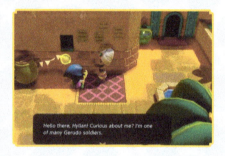

## Tornado Ghost?

Location: Gerudo Town
Reward: Fresh Milk

A reasonably simple one to complete. Just make sure you've already captured an Echo of a *Tornando* (found flying around in a whirl in the nearby open desert).

Simply show her one and she'll give you some **[Fresh Milk]** as thanks.

## Wild Sandstorms

Location: Gerudo Desert
Reward: Gold Sash

First you **must** kill both the *Lanmolas* mini-boss that roams around the North-West part of the desert. Speak with the Gerudo and they'll mention another one. You must kill this - tougher - one found near the Eastern desert entrance. Come back here for the **[Gold Sash]**.

## Dohna's Challenge

Location: Gerudo Town
Reward: Silk Pajamas

**After** completing the *Still Missing* main quest, speak with *Dohna* and then use a *Holmill* Echo to break into the roof of the Treasury!

Once inside you need to sneak your way to the end to claim the **[Pajamas]**. *Pots* and *Strandtulas* are great Echoes to use here!

## Deliver the Grilled Fish

Location: Seesyde Village
Reward: Bubble Kelp

You **must** take the **original** *Grilled Fish* to her son (an Echo of it **won't** work!). You can find her son up North, past a fallen stone pillar.

Be quick if killing enemies as the Fish may get eaten otherwise! Use *Trampolines/Beds* to get up to him. Return to mum for **[10 x Bubble Kelp]**!

## A Treat for My Person

**After** completing the *Still Missing* main quest and the *Questioning the Local Cats side-quest,* put on your cat suit and speak to the cat at the beach.

Give the cat a **Warm Mixed Special Smoothie** and the cat will reward you with a **Might Crystal** in return.

## The Zappy Shipwreck

**After** completing the *Still Missing* main quest, speak with *General Wright* and then head to the wrecked ship in the water. Use **Bind** on the wood and be ready for a mini-dungeon!

We recommend having a few shock-resistant smoothies for this one! For a guide on how to beat the mini-boss, see page 114.

## The Zora Child's Fate

**After** completing the *Chaos at River Zora Village* main quest, speak with the child, then go in the hut to speak with mum.

She needs you to throw the following three Echoes into the water: 1. A *Tangler* 2. A *Bombfish* and 3. A *Biri.* You'll get the **[Zora Scale]** in return!

## Precious Treasure

Location: River Zora Village
Reward: 3 x Monster Stones

After completing the *Rampage in Zora Cove* main quest, speak with this Zora in the village entrance.

Head outside, swim up Northwest and use **Bind** to pull the chest out of the water. Open it, then use **Bind** to take the *empty chest* back to the Zora.

## Out of Bubble Kelp

Location: Seesyde Village
Reward: 20 Rupees

The Smoothie shopkeeper here needs **3 x Bubble Kelp** to open. If you have those already, just hand them over to finish it.

Otherwise, completing the *Grilled Fish Delivery* side quest gives you 10 Bubble Kelp as a reward. Or, buy 4 from the shop. Up to you.

## Big Shot

Location: Zora Cove
Reward: 10 x Riverhorses

Located near the middle of *Lake Zora*, you'll find this guy stuck on top of his boat. You have to clear the surrounding water of enemies to finish this side quest.

We repeatedly used *Bombfish* and **Bound** to hold them in front of us, letting the enemies swim right into them until they were all gone.

## Secret Chief Talks

Location: Zora Cove
Reward: Gold Brooch

**After** completing the *Chaos at Rampage in Zora* main quest, speak with *Rogma*. Head to *Dradd's House* (top of *River Zora*), then head to the top of the waterfalls *East of Zora Village* and speak with *Tellum*.

Look for a cave (with a broken corner) in *Zora* Cove. Speak with *Dradd* for the **[Gold Brooch]**.

## Runaway Horse

Location: Hyrule Ranch
Reward: Free horse use

Speak with the man in *Hyrule Ranch* and then immediately go West and look for the *Horse* stranded in the middle of the small island.

Use some *Old Beds* to create a makeshift platform (to the right side) and then climb on the horse and ride it back to the ranch to unlock the ability to use them anytime!

## Let's Play a Game

Location: Eastern Hyrule Field
Reward: Ancient Charm

This side quest is actually a mini dungeon! Create and use the *Spark* Echoes here to fill the numerous boxes placed throughout (sparks will go straight and follow around objects).

To beat the boss, please see page 81. Warp outside for your prize.

## The Great Fairy's Request

Location: Lake Hylia
Reward: Might Bell

**After** completing the *Rift on Eldin Volcano* main quest & maxing out your accessory capacity speak with *The Great Fairy*.

Great Fairy
But... BUT! To earn it, you'll have to accede to my request.

Now you must: Give the *Gerudo* shop owner an *Unfortunate Smoothie* for a *Floral Seashell*. Speak with the *Goron City* shop keeper, and kill all enemies in the *Lizalfos Burrow* cave for the *Magma Stone*.

Give the stone and the seashell to the *Gerudo* shop keeper for the *Pendant* and give the *Fairy* the *Pendant* for the *Might Bell*!

The cave where you can find magma stones is by the lava lake north of Goron City.

So, do you know about floral seashells and magma stones?

## An Out-There Zol

Location: Hyrule Castle Town
Reward: Heart Piece

After completing the lengthy *Dampé Automation* (see page 156 on how to do that), and the *Curious Child* side quests first, speak with this kid again for this side quest.

There's gotta be a Zol that's really out there! I mean, like, cute AND flashy!

Summon the *Gizmol Automaton* and you'll be rewarded with a **[Heart Piece]** for blowing his curious, little mind! How sweet.

## Impa's Gift

*Location: Hyrule Castle*
*Reward: White Horse*

After completing the *Still Missing* main quest-line, talk to *Impa* in the *Throne Room*. Now go to *Hyrule Ranch* and speak with the girl here.

Head North-east to the rift, beat the rift, then pull out a *Carrot* with **Bind** and the *White Horse* should appear. Pull out another *Carrot* to learn its Echo while you're here.

## One Soldier Too Many

*Location: Hyrule Castle*
*Reward: Golden Egg*

After completing the *Still Missing* main quest-line, talk to the guard at the castle entrance. Now talk to the soldiers:

1. On the wall,
2. In the barracks,
3. By the well.

Talk with *Beecher* in the *Barracks* again to trigger a cut-scene and claim your **[Golden Egg]**.

## From the Heart

*Location: Hyrule Castle Town*
*Reward: Customary Attire*

After completing the *One Soldier Too Many* and *Impa's Gift* side quests, speak with the *Girl* with the dog outside the castle. Now speak with the *King* inside and then head to the *Rift* as shown on the map.

Complete the *Stilled Southern Hyrule Field* Rift to be rewarded with the new outfit.

## Cuccos on the Loose

Location: Kakariko Village
Reward: Fairy Bottle

Talk to the distressed lady outside her home and she'll ask you to return her **five** Cuccos.

The first three are nearby in town. However, the last two are: in the nearby graveyard, *and on top of the windmill*! (Very easy to miss).

Throw them in the pen to finish.

## Questioning the Local Cats

Location: Kakariko Village
Reward: Cat Clothes

After speaking with the *old man*, talk to the woman in front of the shop. Now head to the *Windmill* and use a *Grilled Fish* Echo by the cat to get it to move.

Use a *Holmill* Echo to dig where the cat was for the **[Cat Clothes]**! Put it on, head for the other *Windmill* (by the gravestones), speak with the cat here, and then you'll find the old man's cat outside the village on a tree.

## A Curious Child

Location: Hyrule Castle Town
Reward: Might Crystal

This inquisitive kid wants to see **every** different type of *Zol* there is! Summon up the following *Zol Echoes* for him:

- *Zol*
- *Ignizol*
- *Hydrozol*
- *A BIGGER Hydrozol* (use a *Water Block* Echo to do this.)

## The Fireworks Artist

**Location: Goron City**
**Reward: 50 Rupees**

After getting rid of the *Rifts* on *Eldin Volcano*, speak with *Basa* in the *Goron City*. Now head to the far-East side of the volcano and look for the many **Diamond-shaped Golden Flowers** (near the hot spring).

Pick up the **[Blastpowder Soil]** from the glittering spot and take it back to *Basa* to end this side-quest.

## Ready, Set, Goron!

**Location: Eldin Volcano**
**Reward: 50 Rupees**

After getting rid of the *Rifts* on *Eldin Volcano*, speak with the *Goron* East of *Goron City*. You'll be challenged to a race up the volcano. Luckily, with the right Echoes, you can skip 90% of the course and win super-quickly! Here's how…

Use a *Platboom* behind the start line to go straight up. Go up the slope, then use a *Flying Tile* to the flag to win! MWAHAHAHA! >:D

## Glide Path

**Location: Eldin Volcano**
**Reward: 10 x Rock Salt**

After getting rid of the *Rifts* on *Eldin Volcano*, speak with *Seko* by the cliff edge.

The goal here is to use a flying Echo (such as a *Crow* or a *Peahat*) to glide along the left-side of the volcano to the flag. Just be sure to use the numerous updrafts to stay high enough to make it. Easy.

## Glide Path Trailblazer

Location: Eldin Volcano
Reward: 2 x Might Crystals

Once you've beaten the *Glide Path* side quest, it's time to try the harder version!

Like before, use a flying Echo and use the wind geysers to keep you afloat while you also dodge the falling boulders! Reach the flag to win and grab the **Might Crystals**!

## The Flames of Fortune

Location: Eldin Volcano
Reward: 2 x Might Crystals

After getting rid of the *Rifts* on *Eldin Volcano*, speak with the *Goron* in-between *Rock-Roast Quarry* and *Lizalfos Burrows*.

You need to drag the coal down to *Goron City* entrance whilst keeping it lit (use the lava or lava-enemies to do this). Drop the lava by the *Goron* at the entrance to complete this side quest.

## A Mountainous Mystery

Location: Eldin Volcano
Reward: Goron's Bracelet

After getting rid of the *Rifts* on *Eldin Volcano*, speak with *Darston* in his cave. Ready up your *Lava Rock* Echo and head inside.

Navigate your way past the lava pillars until you reach the mini-boss. Our detailed guide on how to beat it is on page 152. Warp back to *Darston* for the **[Goron Bracelet]**!

## Getting it Twisted

**Location: Hebra Mountain**
**Reward: 10 x Warm Peppers**

Business Scrub

Oh, my dear twisted pumpkin... Where are

This business scrub wants you to show him a *Twisted Pumpkin*. If you have one already, sweet! You're done!

If not though, then use a *Crawtula* to climb up the (high) wall to your right and you'll find one up here in the snow. Immediately warp back and hand it to him.

## Stamp Stand Swallowed

**Location: Hebra Mountain**
**Reward: Stamp Stand**

Once you've activated the *Rift on Mount Lanayru* main quest, speak to *Stamp Man* and enter the Rift.

Tri's friends can be found on the far West, East, and Northern parts of the Rift.

Once they've been rescued, the Stamp Stand is open for you to collect the **Stamp** from!

What, reeeally?

## Snowball Magic

**Location: Conde's House (Hebra Mountain)**
**Reward: Heart Piece**

What to do...

After completing the *Rift on Holy Mount Lanayru* main quest, speak to *Conde*.

The trick here is to use **Bind** on a high-up *Snowball* (the ones right where you appear are perfect), and **carefully** carry it up to the spot where you need to drop it. You can clear the path in advance with fire-based Echoes if it helps.

## The Mythical Deku Snake

Location: Scrubton
Reward: 2 x Monster Stones

After finishing the *Rift in the Faron Wetlands* main quest, talk with the *Deku Scrub* by the *Smoothie Shop*.

Simply give the Scrub **3 x [Electro Apples]** to finish this side quest! You can buy some from the *Hyrule Castle Shop* if need be.

## Mobbing Mothulas

Location: Scrubton
Reward: Might Crystal

After finishing the *Rift in the Faron Wetlands* main quest, pull up the Scrub hiding in the ground and then head to the very South-eastern corner of *Scrubton*.

Use ranged Echoes/Swordfighter form Arrows to take out every *Mothula* and then report back to the Scrub to finish the side quest.

## The Rain-Making Monster

Location: Scrubton
Reward: 8 x Electro Apples

You'll be asked to show this Scrub a *Drippitune*. These are the **Blue Frogs** found all around *Scrubton*.

Once you've cloned one as an Echo, go back to the Scrub and show it to complete this side quest.

## Looking for Bempu

Location: Scrubton
Reward: Fairy Fragrance

**After** completing the *A Rift in the Faron Wetlands* main quest, speak with *Bempu*. You need to use **Bind** to pull him out of the ground from the following four locations:

1. Front of the Smoothie Shop.
2. Top-left corner, heart lake.
3. Top-center (between statues).
4. Bottom-right corner of the map.

## Cotton-Candy Hunt

Location: Scrubton
Reward: Curious Charm

**After** completing the *A Rift in the Faron Wetlands* main quest, and the *Let's Play a Game* side quest, go to area in *Scrubton* with the Deku statue and two unlit *Braziers* nearby. Clear the frogs, then light the Braziers to open a dungeon entrance.

Use a combination of manual *Spark* Echoes and fire to make it through each of the room puzzles. To beat the boss, please see page 187. Go back to the Scrub for your prize!

## Recipes, Please!

Location: Any Smoothie Shop
Reward: Survey Scope/Binoculars

You need to create a total of **30** new recipes from scratch to unlock the best item (the **Binoculars**). See page 18 for the full smoothie list.

Oh, and make sure you have enough Rupees (**300**) as well as ingredients if you want to finish this side quest.

# Side-Quests

The locations of the numerous Side Quests can be found on the map below.

# MINI-GAMES

## Time-Trialing Fun for Everyone!

A Zelda game wouldn't be complete without a handful of mini-games, each one consisting of multiple rounds (with better prizes at stake at each difficulty level), and an on-screen timer to keep your anxiety levels at sufficiently high levels!

And Echoes of Wisdom, is no different. Each mini-game costs **10 Rupees** to play, although you'll always end up with more Rupees as a prize for completing the easiest difficulty courses/challenges.

It's important to note that, no matter how many amazing tips and tricks we give you here, success will ultimately come down to practice and your ability to remain calm under pressure (*especially* when you've got less time to do the same, or more difficult, challenges in).

We'll tell you the easiest ways we found to complete each mini-game at each difficulty.

Best of luck!

## Acorn Gathering

**Location: West of Hyrule Field < 25 Secs Reward: Steel Trap**

Our top tips:

- Use the *Platboom* Echo to reach all of the acorns on the really high platforms.
- The *Frog Ring* will make jumping up onto the smaller walls a breeze.
- Their location *never* changes, so go in a *clockwise* direction.

## Acorn Gathering

Our top tips:

- Spin dash while in the water to swim faster.
- The 5th and 6th acorns are underwater.
- This is the shortest course, so a sub 22-second time is more than do-able.

## Acorn Gathering

Our top tips:

- Use the *Platboom* Echo for getting up onto the trees.
- Spin dash when you're on the ground
- Only 11 acorns are needed, so a sub 20-second time is very achievable.

## Acorn Gathering

Our top tips:

- Use the *Platboom* Echo for reaching the acorn on the high platform in front of you.
- Collect the acorn by the waterfall next, then collect the rest in an anti-clockwise fashion.
- Use a trampoline on the lily-pad to reach the tree.

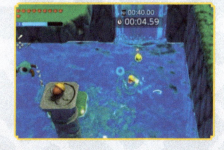

## Acorn Gathering

**Location: Northern Sanctuary**
**Reward: Golden Egg**

Our top tips:

- Switch to Swordfighter mode and jump onto the left-hand ledge.
- Jump off the ledge by the top to get the acorn on the hedge.
- Use a *Platboom* at the front of the church to grab the acorn on the roof last.

## Mango Rush

**Difficulty: Standard Seeds**
**Reward: Up to 5 Tough Mangoes**

Our top tips:

- The mangoes appear in the same order for each difficulty (so they can be learned)!
- Use the *Frog Ring* or *Two Tables* to get onto the upper ledge.
- Spin dash all the way through to make it easier to hit **50** mangoes before they stop growing.

## Mango Rush

**Difficulty: Vibrant Seeds**
**Reward: Golden Fan**

Our top tips:

- Spikes now grow, meaning you need to learn where they pop up out of the ground.
- Harvesting 50-59 seeds nets you the **[Golden Fan]**. Harvesting all 60 earns you **3 x [Might Crystals]**.

## Mango Rush

**Difficulty: Ultimate Seeds**
**Reward: Dancing Outfit**

Our top tips:

- Bomb plants will now appear. You *can* set these off to take out some of the mangoes.
- Harvesting 60-69 seeds nets you the **[Dancing Outfit]**. Harvesting all 70 earns you a **[Piece of Heart]**.

## Flag Race (Short)

**Location: Hyrule Ranch**
**< 17 - 23 secs Reward: 6 x Might Crystals**

Our top tips:

- To get under 17-seconds, dash at the beginning of the race and then *immediately* after coming out of a corner.
- This is a, relatively, quick way of earning up to a whopping 6 **x Might Crystals**!

## Flag Race (Medium)

**Location: Hyrule Ranch**
**< 20 secs Reward: Piece of Heart**

Our top tips:

- You can take advantage of the fact that you don't have to be 100% precise with the flags (allowing you to cut corners ever-so-slightly).
- Keep your turns tight here.
- A 20 - 25 second time earns you the **[Pristine Music Box]**.

## Flag Race (Long)

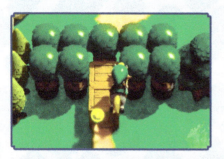

Our top tips:

- This combines the path of both courses into one.
- You can take a shortcut after the third flag by jumping on the boxes to get over the trees.
- Dash out of the tight corners to make the < 40 secs target.

# Slumber Dojo

This is a surprisingly long and involved mini-game that's spread out over a total of **15** different timed battles.

Not only will you need to defeat every enemy in each stage to proceed to the next one, but each one will have its own set of rules (such as starting out with zero Echoes learned).

Let's take a look at the key milestone rewards you get for completing a set number.

This is on top of the rewards you get for finishing the challenge, which can be for either beating it outright, or clearing it super quick.

| Milestone | Reward |
|---|---|
| Clear 2 stages | Piece of Heart |
| Clear 4 stages | First Mastery Accessory |
| Clear 6 stages | Heirloom Katana |
| Clear 8 stages | Second Mastery Accessory |
| Clear 11 stages | Piece of Heart |
| Clear 14 stages | Final Mastery Accessory |

## Blank-Slate Battle

Our top tips:

- Use the rock on both the *Octorok, Moblin*, and the *Keese*.
- Use **Bind** on the *Deku Baba* and then pull it back to quickly finish this level with the minimum of hassle.

## Caromadillos' Revenge

Our top tips:

- Throw out a *Peahat* and let it roll around while you switch to *Swordfighter* mode.
- Do quick spin attacks (rotate joystick 360 degrees + attack) to take out the remaining enemies ASAP.

## Flow of Battle

Our top tips:

- It's best to use an Echo with a long-range attack, such as a *Wizzrobe*. However, a *Peahat* can also be effective.
- Use a *Flying Tile* to navigate around the room *much* faster than using the boards in the water.

## Blank-Slate Battle: Wind

**Time Limit: 1:05**
**Reward: 5 x Chilly Cactus**

Our top tips:
- A super easy way to finish this level quickly is to use **Bind** on all but one of the enemies.
- Carry them to the hole in the middle and drop them in!
- Use the *wind-cannon* to clear the sand and drop the final enemy in to win!

## Titans' Gathering

**Time Limit: 10:00**
**Reward: 5 x Fresh Milk**

Our top tips:
- This is a boss rush mode where you'll fight one boss right after another.
- For *Seismic Talus* see page 47
- For *Vocavor* see page 100
- For *Mogryph* see page 74

With our strats, this will be easy.

## Moblins' Revenge

**Time Limit: 1:00**
**Reward: 20 Rupees**

Our top tips:
- You've got access to all of your Echoes, so pick your strongest one.
- We used a *Sword Moblin Lv. 3*, but if you don't have one, a *Peahat* or any other multi-hit Echo will work.

## Floating on Fire

Our top tips:

- Pick a *Wizzrobe* (not the fire one!) or and *Ice Octo* and eliminate all enemies from the top of the room to the bottom.
- You can speed things up using *Swordfighter* form as well.

## A Shock in the Dark

Our top tips:

- We highly recommend bringing a *Sword Moblin Lv. 3* with you here as it'll kill all *Sparks* quickly.
- Use *Braziers* to light up the room.
- Use a platform to reach the last enemy at the end.

## Blank-Slate Battle: Ice

Our top tips:

- Use **Bind** to drag and drop the enemies into the abyss!
- Be weary if you're not wearing any appropriate footwear before starting the battle, as it's very slippery!
- You won't lose health going in the abyss, so you can take those enemies with you!

## Revenge from the Skies

**Time Limit: 1:10**
**Reward: 8 x Twisted Pumpkins**

**Our top tips:**

- We recommend you use a long-range Echo such as *Spear Moblin Lv. 2*, or any *Wizzrobes* if you have them available.
- Keep locking and dodging and let the Echoes do the hard work for you here.

## Blank-Slate Battle: Final

**Time Limit: 2:00**
**Reward: 3 x Golden Eggs**

**Our top tips:**

- Use the *Rock* to get the *Keese*, and use those to get the *Fire Octo*.
- Use this as a molten-turret and use them to clear the bottom floor *first*.
- Once that's clear, use the wind to go up to the upper floor. Clear using the *Fire Octos*.

## Trial of Flame and Ice

**Time Limit: 0:55**
**Reward: 5 x Golden Eggs**

**Our top tips:**

- Hopefully you'll have the *Sword Moblin Lv. 3* that we've recommended for a few of these challenges.
- Keep spamming it as it'll take (and deal) decent punishment before expiring.

## Wizzrobe Gathering

Time Limit: 2:35
Reward: 50 Rupees

Our top tips:

- This can be frustrating. We recommend using either opposing *Wizzrobes* (so Fire on Ice for example), or using opposing *Octos* and carrying them around while locking on to each target, one at a time.

## The Titans Gather Again

Time Limit: 10:45
Reward: 5 x Monster Stones

Our top tips:

- This is a boss rush mode where you'll fight one boss right after another.
- For *Volvagia* see page 148
- For *Gohma* see page 183
- For *Skorchill* see page 209

## The Titans' Final Gathering

Time Limit: 15:50
Reward: The Green Tunic

The final battle..

- You'll face off against the same 6 bosses you've fought before.
- However, you'll now also have to face *Ganon* at the end!
- Nip in and out of *Swordfighter* mode as you dodge the *Fire Keese* and get close enough to hit Ganon. Hit him enough to win!

# Mini-Games

The mini-game locations have been labeled as follows:

**Acorns**    **Flag Race**    **Mango Rush**    **Slumber Dojo**

# EASTER EGGS

## Shhh! Can You Keep a Secret?

As you'd expect being made by the same developers as the Link's Awakening Remake, there's *loads* of obvious - and some not so obvious - references to past Zelda/Nintendo games hidden throughout the game. How many of these did you spot?…

### Link's House

There's **loads** of past Zelda references stuffed outside Link's house in Kakariko Village, as well as inside. Let's take a close look…

### Marin's Flower

The **red flower** on top of Link's house is the same flower that *Marin* wears in her hair in Link's Awakening!

### Inside Link's House

There's quite a few references littered around Link's abandoned bedroom…

- Link's hat (by his bed),
- The Wooden Owl (used to warp around in past games),
- The books are the same colors used on the official *Hyrule Historia, Encyclopedia, and Art & Artifact* books published by Nintendo,
- The *Green Rug* is the same one found under Link's bed in the **Minish Cap** GBA games,
- Finally, the potions are a reference to the ones found beside Link's bed in **Skyward Sword**.

## Echoes and Voices

Those annoying (but cute looking) *Pols-Voice* creatures from *Link's Awakening* show up as a stuffed toy in one of the houses in *Hyrule Castle Town*.

## Link's Hood and Shield

*Tears of the Kingdom/Breath of the Wild* fans may well recognize the hood as the one worn in both of those games (as well as the shield used in both of those games).

## Battle with Ganon

The initial battle against Ganon is a nod to the final battle in the *Link to the Past* game on the Super Nintendo.

Not only does Ganon have a Trident in the SNES version, but he also fires out *Fire Keese* at you like in Echoes of Wisdom. How neat is that?!

## Goddess Statue

The statue that Zelda changes behind at the start of the game resembles the *Goddess Statue* from **Skyward Sword** and this is the deity that became reincarnated as Zelda herself…

# ITEM TABLES

 ## For All You 100% Fans...

Over the following pages you'll find our reference tables for the accessories, clothing, and every single Echo found in the game.

Finally, we've gone all-in on the overworld maps and split them into key groups, to make the guides as easy-to-read as possible.

Each map shows you:

1. All **28** Accessory Locations
2. All Clothing you can unlock
3. All Shop locations and what they sell
4. All **127** Echo Locations
5. All **40** Pieces of Heart Locations
6. All **150** Might Crystals Locations
7. All **25** Stamp Stand & **6** Smoothie Shop Locations

| Item Table | Page No |
|---|---|
| Accessories (+ Map) | 255 |
| Clothing | 260 |
| Shops | 261 |
| Non-Enemy Echoes | 262 |
| Enemy Echoes | 266 |

| Map | Page No |
|---|---|
| Pieces of Heart | 276 |
| Might Crystals | 278 |
| Stamp Stands & Smoothie Shops | 280 |

# ACCESSORIES

There's a total of **28** Accessories to find. You'll need a total of 1900 Rupees to unlock all available accessory slots from the *Great Fairy*.

| Name | Icon | Benefits | How to Get |
|------|------|----------|------------|
| *Ancient Charm* | | Reduces damage taken | Complete the *Let's Play a Game* side-quest |
| *Charging Horn* | | Horses can charge forwards for longer | Clear the *Long Course* of the *Flag Race* in **under 40 seconds** |
| *Climbing Band* | | Climb ladders and rock walls faster | Buy for **500 Rupees** from *Kakariko Shop* |
| *Clockwork Bangle* | | Wind up Clockwork keys faster | Help Dampé build **all six** Automatons |
| *Curious Charm* | | Reduces damage taken | Complete the *Cotton Candy Hunt* side-quest |
| *Energy Belt* | | Improved odds of more energy appearing after dark monster fights | In a guarded chest in a *Hebra Mountain* cave |
| *Energy Glove* | | Even better odds of more energy appearing | In a guarded chest, N/W of *Gerudo Desert* |
| *Fairy Flower* | | Improved odds of fairy's appearing from cut grass | In a N/W cave near the bottom of *Eldin Volcano* |
| *Fairy Fragrance* | | Even better odds of fairy's appearing from cut grass | Complete the *Looking for Bempo* side-quest |

| Name | Icon | Benefits | How to Get |
|------|------|----------|------------|
| *Final Mastery* | | Stay in Swordfighter form the longest | Complete all **14** *Slumber Dojo* training sessions |
| *First Mastery* | | Stay in Swordfighter form for longer | Complete **4** *Slumber Dojo* training sessions |
| *Frog Ring* | | Allows you to jump as high as the sword-form any time | In a chest on floor **B2** of *Hyrule Castle* |
| *Gerudo Sandals* | | Stops you from sinking in the dark quicksand | Costs **400 Rupees** from the *Gerudo Shop* |
| *Gold Brooch* | | Rupees are far more likely to appear from objects/enemies | Complete the *Secret Chief Talks* side-quest |
| *Gold Sash* | | Stops you from being blown around by high winds | Complete the *Wild Sandstorms* side-quest |
| *Goron's Bracelet* | | You won't slow down when carrying objects | Complete the *A Mountainous Mystery* side-quest |
| *Heart Barrette* | | Small hearts more likely to appear | Complete the *Beetle Ballyhoo* side-quest |
| *Heart Pin* | | Small hearts even more likely to appear | In a chest on the 2nd floor of *Suthorn Ruins* |
| *Ice Spikes* | | Allows you to walk normally on ice | In a guarded cave, West of *Hebra Mountain* |

| Name | Icon | Benefits | How to Get |
|------|------|----------|------------|
| *Might Bell* | | Rings when you're near a Might Crystal | Complete the *Great Fairy's Request* side-quest |
| *Second Mastery* | | Stay in Swordfighter form for even longer | Complete **8** *Slumber Dojo* training sessions |
| *Silver Brooch* | | Rupees are more likely to appear from objects/enemies | In a chest behind a bomb-able wall, West of *River Zora Waypoint* |
| *Spin Brace* | | Spin into enemies to knock them back | In a guarded cave, N/E side of *Scrubton* |
| *Stone Anklet* | | Reduces how much you're knocked back | Costs **400 Rupees** from *Hyrule Castle Town Shop* |
| *Survey Binoculars* | | Smoothie Ingredients and Monster Stones are much more likely to appear | Make **30 different** Smoothies |
| *Survey Scope* | | Smoothie Ingredients and Monster Stones are more likely to appear | Make **10 different** smoothies |
| *Zora Scale* | | Greatly increases how long you can stay underwater | Complete the *Zora Child's Fate* side-quest |
| *Zora's Flippers* | | Swim/spin faster in water | Costs **350 Rupees** from the *River Zora Shop* |

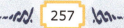

# ACCESSORIES MAP

Below you'll find the in-game map with the locations for all 28 Accessories in the game. Don't forget to max out your accessory slots (five) by buying them from the Great Fairy.

# CLOTHING

There's a total of 11 sets of clothes to find. Let's take a look at what benefits they offer (other than looking cool), and how/where to get them.

| Name | Icon | Benefits | Location |
|---|---|---|---|
| Black Cat Clothes | | Allows you to speak to the cats | Scan any *Ganon Amiibo* (random drop) |
| Blue Attire | | Look Pretty | Scan any *Zelda Amiibo* (random drop) |
| Cat Clothes | | Allows you to speak to the cats | Do the *Local Cats* Side Quest in Kakariko Village |
| Dancing Outfit | | Wider spin circle | Complete the hardest *Mango Rush* round |
| Green Tunic | | Look more like Link | Complete 15 *Slumber Dojo* Mini-game Challenges |
| Red Tunic | | Look more like a red version of Link | Scan any *Link Amiibo* (random drop) |
| Royal Travel Attire | | Look more like Zelda as you know her | Complete the *Hyrule Castle Dungeon* Quest |
| Silk Pajamas | | Recover hearts faster while in bed | Complete *Dohna's Challenge* Side-Quest (See page 225) |
| Stamp Suit | | "STAMP!" *Fist pump* | Collect all 25 *Stamps* (See page 280) |

# SHOPS

| Name | Items for Sale (+ Rupee Cost) |
|---|---|
| Gerudo Shop | • *Gerudo Sandals (400)*<br>• *Warm Pepper (50)*<br>• *Chilly Cactus (30)*<br>• *Red Potion (30)* |
| Goron Shop | • *Rocktato (25)*<br>• *Rock Salt (30)*<br>• *Red Potion (30)*<br>• *Blue Potion (30)* |
| Hyrule Castle Town Shop | • *Stone Anklet (400)*<br>• *Radiant Butter (50)*<br>• *Electro Apple (30)*<br>• *Red Potion (30)* |
| Kakariko Village Shop | • *Climbing Band (500)*<br>• *Refreshing Grapes (40)*<br>• *Red Potion (30)*<br>• *Purple Potion (50)* |
| Milk Shop<br>(inside *Hyrule Ranch*) | • *Fresh Milk (50)* |
| River Zora Shop | • *Zora's Flippers (350)*<br>• *Riverhorse (40)*<br>• *Red Potion (30)*<br>• *Blue Potion (30)* |
| Sea Zora's Shop | • *Bubble Kelp (25)*<br>• *Red Potion (30)*<br>• *Blue Potion (30)* |
| Seesyde Village Shop | • *Red Potion (30)*<br>• *Blue Potion (30)*<br>• *Purple Potion (50)* |
| Suthorn Village Shop | • *Piece of Heart (80)*<br>• *Floral Nectar (30)*<br>• *Red Potion (30)*<br>• *Purple Potion (50)* |

# Non-Enemy Echoes

There's a total of **34** Non-Enemy Echoes to find throughout the game. These Echoes are most often used to solve puzzles/as platforms.

| Name | Icon | Cast Cost | Location | Learned? |
|------|------|-----------|----------|----------|
| Ancient Orb | | 1x | Eternal Forest (after the Prime Energy) | ☐ |
| Beetle Mound | | 3x | N/E cave, Gerudo Desert | ☐ |
| Boulder | | 1x | In an Eastern cave, Faron Wetlands | ☐ |
| Brazier | | 2x | Inside a cave, Suthorn Forest | ☐ |
| Carrot | | 1x | Carrot patch, N/W of Hyrule Castle | ☐ |
| Cat Statue | | 1x | Gerudo Sanctum Dungeon | ☐ |
| Cloud | | 2x | Stilled Hebra Mountain | ☐ |
| Decorative Shrub | | 1x | Beginning of the game (Hyrule Castle Prison) | ☐ |
| Elephant Statue | | 1x | Gerudo Sanctum Dungeon | ☐ |

| Name | Icon | Cast Cost | Location | Learned? |
|------|------|-----------|----------|----------|
| Firework | | 2x | Eldin Volcano (after a side-quest) | |
| Flying Tile | | 3x | N/W cave in Gerudo Desert | |
| Gerudo Pot | | 1x | Gerudo Town | |
| Grilled Fish | | 1x | Seesyde Village | |
| Hawk Statue | | 1x | Gerudo Sanctum Dungeon | |
| Hyrule Castle Pot | | 1x | Hyrule Castle | |
| Ice Block | | 1x | Most caves, Hebra Mountain | |
| Lava Rock | | 4x | Eldin Volcano | |
| Meat | | 1x | Suthorn Forest | |
| Old Bed | | 1x | Start of the game | |

| Name | Icon | Cast Cost | Location | Learned? |
|------|------|-----------|----------|----------|
| Pot | | 1x | Most Hyrule homes | |
| Rock | | 1x | Suthorn Beach | |
| Rock Roast | | 1x | Inside Rock-Roast Quarry, Eldin Volcano | |
| Sign | | 1x | All around Hyrule | |
| Snake Statue | | 1x | Gerudo Sanctum Dungeon | |
| Snowball | | 2x | Upper Hebra Mountain | |
| Soft Bed | | 2x | Oasis Tent, Gerudo Desert | |
| Spiked Roller | | 4x | S/W Corner cave of the Eternal Forest | |
| Stuffed Toy | | 1x | In a cave, under the large gravestone, near Hyrule Castle | |
| Table | | 1x | At the beginning of the game | |

| Name | Icon | Cast Cost | Location | Learned? |
|------|------|-----------|----------|----------|
| Trampoline |  | 1x | Suthorn Village well | ☐ |
| Water Block | | 1x | Stilled Jabu Waters | ☐ |
| Wind Cannon | | 2x | Eastern Cave, near Gerudo Sanctum | ☐ |
| Wooden Block | | 1x | At the start of the game | ☐ |
| Zelda's Bed | | 3x | Zelda' Room, Hyrule Castle | ☐ |

# ENEMY ECHOES

There's a total of **93** Enemy Echoes to find throughout the game. Some of the coolest ones won't appear until the end so, remember that.

| Name | Icon | Cast Cost | Location | Learned? |
|------|------|-----------|----------|----------|
| Albatrawl | | 2x | Zora Cove | |
| Armos | | 2x | In an Eastern Cave, Faron Wetlands | |
| Aruroda | | 2x | Gerudo Desert | |
| Baby Ghoma | | 2x | West Faron Wetlands | |
| Ball-and-Chain Trooper | | 4x | Stilled Hyrule Castle | |
| Beakon | | 3x | Faron Wetlands | |
| Beamos | | 3x | Inside a cave, Faron Wetlands | |
| Beetle | | 1x | Inside a cave, N/E of Gerudo Town | |
| Bio Deku Baba | | 3x | Inside the Wrecked Ship | |

| Name | Icon | Cast Cost | Location | Learned? |
|---|---|---|---|---|
| Biri | | 2x | South-East of Zora Cove | |
| Bombfish | | 4x | In a cave N/W of Lord Jabu Jabu's Den | |
| Boomerang Boarblin | | 2x | N/W Gerudo Desert | |
| Boomerang Boarblin Lv. 2 | | 4x | N/W Gerudo Desert | |
| Buzz Blob | | 3x | Faron Wetlands | |
| Caromadillo | | 2x | Eastern Hyrule Field | |
| Caromadillo Lv. 2 | | 3x | Eastern Hyrule Field | |
| Chompfin | | 4x | Swimming by the Wrecked Ship | |
| Club Boarblin | | 2x | N/W Gerudo Desert | |
| Club Boarblin Lv. 2 | | 4x | N/W Gerudo Desert | |

| Name | Icon | Cast Cost | Location | Learned? |
|------|------|-----------|----------|----------|
| Crawtula | | 3x | By the pillar, Suthorn Prairie | |
| Crow | | 2x | Gerudo Desert Entrance | |
| Darknut | | 3x | Suthorn Ruins | |
| Darknut Lv. 2 | | 4x | Stilled Hyrule Castle | |
| Darknut Lv. 3 | | 5x | End of Faron Wetlands Cave | |
| Deku Baba | | 2x | Suthorn Ruins | |
| Deku Baba Lv. 2 | | 3x | Faron Wetlands South Passageway | |
| Drippitune | | 3x | Faron Wetlands | |
| Electric Keese | | 4x | Stilled Faron Wetlands | |
| Electric Wizzrobe | | 5x | S/E Faron Wetlands | |

| Name | Icon | Cast Cost | Location | Learned? |
|------|------|-----------|----------|----------|
| Fire Keese | | 4x | Inside Summit Cave, Eldin Volcano | |
| Fire Octo | | 2x | Eldin Volcano (outside) | |
| Fire Wizzrobe | | 5x | Eldin Volcano (outside) | |
| Freezard | | 3x | Hebra Mountains | |
| Freeze Slug | | 3x | Lanayru Temple | |
| Ghini | | 1x | Graveyard, North of Hyrule Castle | |
| Ghini Lv. 2 | | 3x | Graveyard, North of Hyrule Castle | |
| Ghirro | | 2x | Inside a cave, Eldin Volcano Trail | |
| Giant Goponga Flower | | 4x | Faron Wetlands | |
| Gibdo | | 3x | Cryptic Cavern, Gerudo Desert | |

| Name | Icon | Cast Cost | Location | Learned? |
|------|------|-----------|----------|----------|
| Gibdo Lv. 2 | | 4x | Cryptic Cavern, Gerudo Desert | |
| Goo Specter | | 3x | East Faron Wetlands | |
| Guay | | 3x | Hyrule Field | |
| Gustmaster | | 3x | Stilled Hyrule Castle | |
| Hoarder | | 3x | Faron Wetlands | |
| Holmill | | 3x | Ancestor's Cave of Rest, Gerudo Desert | |
| Hydrozol | | 2x | Faron Wetlands | |
| Ice Keese | | 4x | Hebra Mountain | |
| Ice Octo | | 2x | Hebra Mountain | |
| Ice Wizzrobe | | 5x | Hebra Mountain | |

| Name | Icon | Cast Cost | Location | Learned? |
|---|---|---|---|---|
| Ignizol | | 2x | Suthorn Forest Caves | ☐ |
| Keese | | 1x | Beach Cave, Suthorn Beach | ☐ |
| Leever | | 2x | Hebra Mountain | ☐ |
| Lizalfos | | 3x | Eldin Volcano (outside) | ☐ |
| Lizalfos Lv. 2 | | 4x | N/W Corner, Eldin Volcano | ☐ |
| Lizalfos Lv. 3 | | 5x | In an underwater cave, West Faron Wetlands | ☐ |
| Lynel | | 6x | Eternal Forest | ☐ |
| Mini-Moldorm | | 2x | Eldin Volcano Trail | ☐ |
| Moa | | 3x | Hebra Mountain | ☐ |
| Mothula | | 3x | Gerudo Sanctum Dungeon | ☐ |

| Name | Icon | Cast Cost | Location | Learned? |
|---|---|---|---|---|
| Mothula Lv. 2 | | 5x | S/E Corner, Faron Wetlands | |
| Needlefly | | 2x | Faron Wetlands | |
| Octorok | | 1x | Suthorn Prairie | |
| Pathblade | | 1x | Cryptic Cavern, Gerudo Desert | |
| Peahat | | 3x | Inside a cave, Suthorn Forest | |
| Piranha | | 2x | Faron Wetlands | |
| Platboom | | 3x | Inside a cave near Gerudo Town | |
| Poe | | 4x | Gerudo Sanctum Dungeon | |
| ReDead | | 3x | Gerudo Desert | |
| Ribbitune | | 2x | East of the Northern Sanctuary | |

| Name | Icon | Cast Cost | Location | Learned? |
|------|------|-----------|----------|----------|
| Rope | | 1x | In the Suthorn Forest tall grass | |
| Sand Crab | | 1x | West of Seesyde Village | |
| Sand Piranha | | 2x | Gerudo Desert | |
| Sea Urchin | | 1x | Suthorn Beach | |
| Snomaul | | 3x | Hebra Mountain | |
| Spark | | 2x | Eastern Temple | |
| Spear Moblin | | 2x | Suthorn Prairies | |
| Spear Moblin Lv. 2 | | 4x | Eternal Forest | |
| Strandtula | | 2x | Suthorn Ruins Stilled Forest | |
| Sword Moblin | | 2x | East Suthorn Forest | |

| Name | Icon | Cast Cost | Location | Learned? |
|------|------|-----------|----------|----------|
| Sword Moblin Lv. 2 | | 4x | Eastern Hyrule Field | |
| Sword Moblin Lv. 3 | | 5x | Eternal Forest | |
| Tangler | | 1x | Lake Hylia | |
| Tangler Lv. 2 | | 2x | N/E from the Sea Zora Village | |
| Tektite | | 2x | Lake Hylia | |
| Tektite Lv. 2 | | 3x | Hebra Mountain | |
| Tweelus | | 2x | In a cave in Eldin Volcano | |
| Temper Tweelus | | 3x | In the cave between Eldin Volcano & Hebra Mountain | |
| Torch Slug | | 3x | Eldin Volcano (around the climbable walls) | |
| Tornando | | 2x | Gerudo Desert | |

| Name | Icon | Cast Cost | Location | Learned? |
|------|------|-----------|----------|----------|
| White Wolfos |  | 5x | Hebra Mountain | |
| Wolfos | | 3x | Hebra Mountain | |
| Zirro | | 3x | Eldin Volcano (outside) | |
| Zol | | 1x | Suthorn Beach | |

# PIECES OF HEART

Eldin Volcano

Page 153

Page 141

Eternal Forest

Page 134

Page 142

Page 128

Page 130

Page 111

Hyrule Cas

Page 134

Page 131

Page 212

Page 124

Page 134

Page 161

Page 122

Page 128

Hyrule Fi

A Set Pi

Page 122

Page 59

Page 52

Suthorn Pra

Page 119

Gerudo Deser

Page 58

Page 37

Page 119

Page 36

Page 56

Page 36

Below you'll find the in-game map with not only the **40 Pieces of Heart** locations placed right where you'll find them in-game, but we also note the page number in our guide where you'll find the solution needed to acquire it (as some are in caves or in dungeons).

# MIGHT CRYSTALS

Below you'll find the in-game map with all **150 Might Crystal** locations placed right where you'll find them in-game. However, please note that, due to the sheer number of them (and the fact that some of them come in multiples of between 2 - 5), that we can't add the page numbers and keep the map legible. Our apologies, but remember you can tick them off throughout the main guide.

et Pin

Eldin Volcano

Page 150

Page 142

Eternal Forest

Page 140

Page 191

Page 138

Hyrule Cas

Page 134

Page 129

Hyrule Field

Page 62

Page 122

Suthorn Pra

Gerudo Desert

Page 59

Su

Page 57

Page 56

Below you'll find the map with not only the **25 Stamp Stand** locations placed right where you'll find them in-game, but we also note what page they are on in the main guide. The jar icons also show you where the **Smoothie Stores** are.

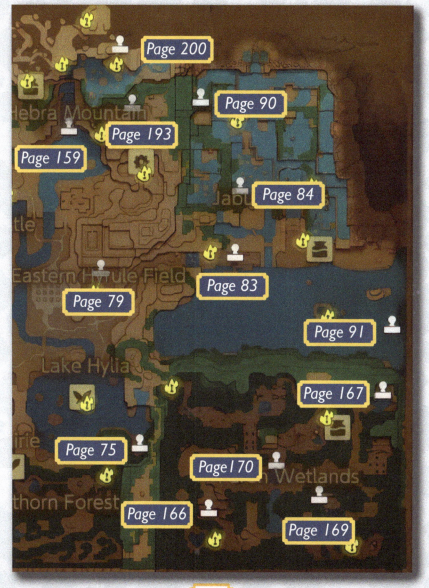

Page 200

Page 90

Page 193

Page 159

Page 84

Page 83

Page 79

Page 91

Page 167

Page 75

Page 170

Page 166

Page 169

# ALSO AVAILABLE!

## Our Other Strategy Guides

**+ASG** Alpha Strategy Guides — **Professional Strategy Guide**

**2nd Edition**

THE LEGEND OF **ZELDA** TEARS OF THE KINGDOM

100% Unofficial - 100% Helpful™

We worked tirelessly to update and revise our biggest strategy guide to-date.

Our 348 page guide to the Tears of the Kingdom covers the entire main story-line from start-to-finish, the solutions to all 152 Shrines, all side adventures, boss guides, Korok Seed locations, data tables galore, and a *whole lot more*.

So, don't miss out on our guide to the biggest game Zelda game so far!

## Available on Amazon now!

Alpha Strategy Guides presents the 3rd Edition of the No. 1 selling and highest-reviewed unofficial strategy guide to Link's Awakening, also on the Switch.

Our comprehensive guide helps you to overcome every challenge, defeat every enemy and boss, locate every secret (including every Heart Piece and Secret Seashell), uncover every hidden Easter Egg, and so much more!

## Available on Amazon now!

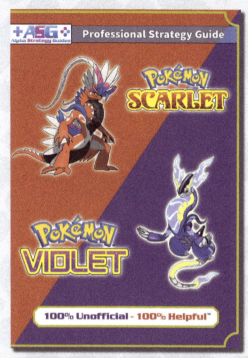

The No. 1 selling (and rated) Metroid Dread strategy guide provides you with expert strategies from a veteran Metroid player and it's now the top-selling and highest rated Metroid Dread guide available!

Defeat every boss, master every move, locate every Missile pack, E-Tank, Power Bomb, and suit upgrade.

Break the game wide open with developer-intended (and very unintentional) sequence breaks, speedruns, and a whole lot more!

## Available on Amazon now!

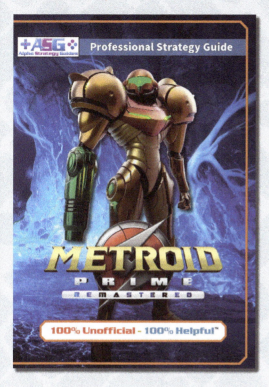

**The classic Metroid Prime got an unexpected remaster in February 2023.**

Our comprehensive guide, authored by a veteran Metroid Prime player, not only shows you how to beat every boss (on Hard difficulty), collect every item, and obtain every scan, but it also shows you how to sequence break the game and play it in a way you've never experienced before.

You definitely won't want to miss this guide!

# Available on Amazon now!

# Thank you for reading!

Please don't forget to leave a review.

We genuinely read them all and take all suggestions into consideration.

Best wishes,

**The Alpha Strategy Guides team.**

Printed in the USA
CPSIA information can be obtained
at www.ICGtesting.com
CBHW051113051224
18497CB00009B/111